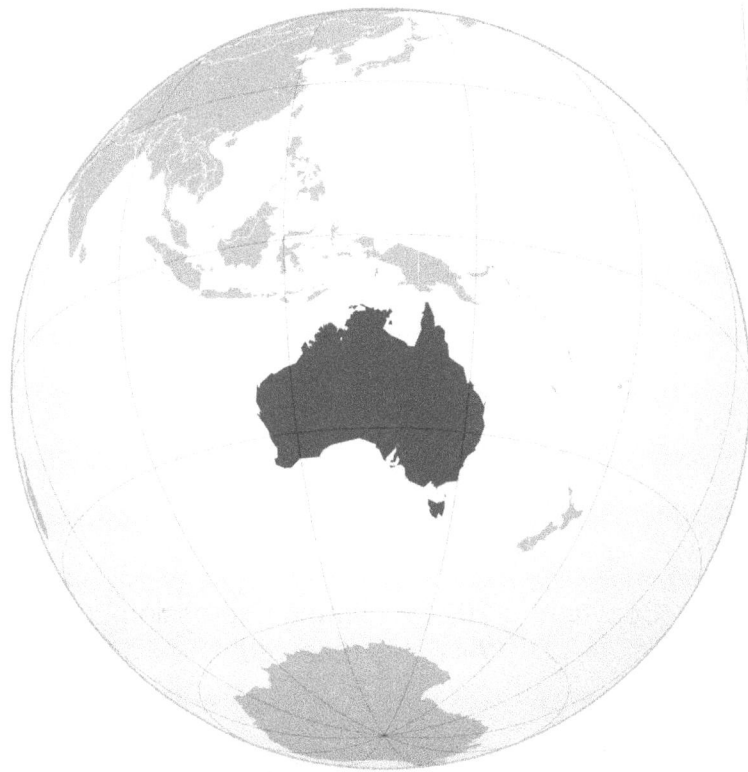

My World (Australia, Oceana and the Poles) Factbook

A Workbook that encompasses the Whole World and its Oceans.

By Brandy Champeau

Exploring Expression

ISBN-13: 978-1-954057-08-1

A note about this Factbook

The World (Australia, Oceana and the Poles) Geography Factbook is a workbook. While there are a number of YouTube videos listed *(and I encourage you to watch them all)* it is **up to you, the learner**, to complete the pages and build your factbook. This means that while many of the aspects will be similar, your finished product will not necessarily look like your neighbors.

My World (Australia, Oceana and the Poles) Geography Factbook will be what **you** make it – a comprehensive keepsake guide created by you as you learn about all of the wonderful biomes, oceans, continents and countries that make up our world.

The Earth

Books about Earth

1. (Y) *Earth: My First 4.5 Billion Years* by Stacy McAnulty and David Litchfield

2. (Y) *Here we are: Notes for Living on Planet Earth* by Oliver Jeffers

3. (Y) *My Friend Earth* by Patricia MacLachlan and Francesca Sanna

4. (O) *The Uninhabitable Earth: Life After Warming* by David Wallace Wells

5. (Y) *The Magic Schoolbus: Inside the Earth* by Joanna Cole

6. (Y) *Under your feet: Soil, sand and Everything Underground* by the Royal Horticultural Society

7. (O) *The Planet in a Petal* by Jan Zalasiewicz

* (O) books are for older readers; (Y) books are for younger readers

Games about Earth

1. Blue Orange Games Planet Board Game

2. Ecos: First Continent

3. Blue Orange Games Photosynthesis Board Game

4. Explore The World

5. Earth Science Bingo

6. Trekking The World

7. BrainBox: All Around the World

8. Earthopoly

9. EcoFluxx

10. It's a Green Life

11. BioViva

Movies about Earth

1.   Earth (G)(2007)

2.   Into the Inferno (2016)

3.   Planet Earth II (2016)

4.   Human planet (2011)

5.   The Salt of the Earth (2014)

6.   Blue Planet (1990)

7.   Secrets of Life (1956)

8.   Wall-E (2008)

9.   Racing Extinction (2015)

10. Earth: One Amazing Day (G)(2017)

YouTube videos about Earth General

- Everything You Need to Know About Planet Earth
  - https://www.youtube.com/watch?v=JGXi_9A__Vc
- The History of Earth - How Our Planet Formed - Full Documentary HD
  - https://www.youtube.com/watch?v=uHUTbq-j0UU
- The World In 2050 [The Real Future Of Earth] - BBC & Nat Geo Documentaries
  - https://www.youtube.com/watch?v=g_1oiJqE3OI
- How the BBC makes Planet Earth look like a Hollywood Movie
  - https://www.youtube.com/watch?v=qAOKOJhzYXk
- BBC Earth's Best Of The Decade | BBC Earth
  - https://www.youtube.com/watch?v=tuVVBnA2lVQ
- Planet Earth: How Mankind is Threatening Life on Earth
  - https://www.youtube.com/watch?v=_t5qQz-91GU
- Earth Facts!
  - https://www.youtube.com/watch?v=YmswDebuZ7c

Planet Fact File: Earth

FACTS

Human Population:_____

Area: _____

Highest Point: _____

Longest River: _____

Tallest Waterfall: _____

Number of Countries: _____

Largest Country: _____

Smallest Country: _____

Number Of Animal Species _____

Largest Land Animal _____

Largest Aquatic Animal _____

Largest Bird _____

Earth's Continents

1:_____

2: _____

3: _____

4: _____

5: _____

6: _____

7: _____

Earth's Oceans

1:_____

2: _____

3: _____

4: _____

5: _____

The Third Rock from the Sun

Label each of the planets in order from the sun.

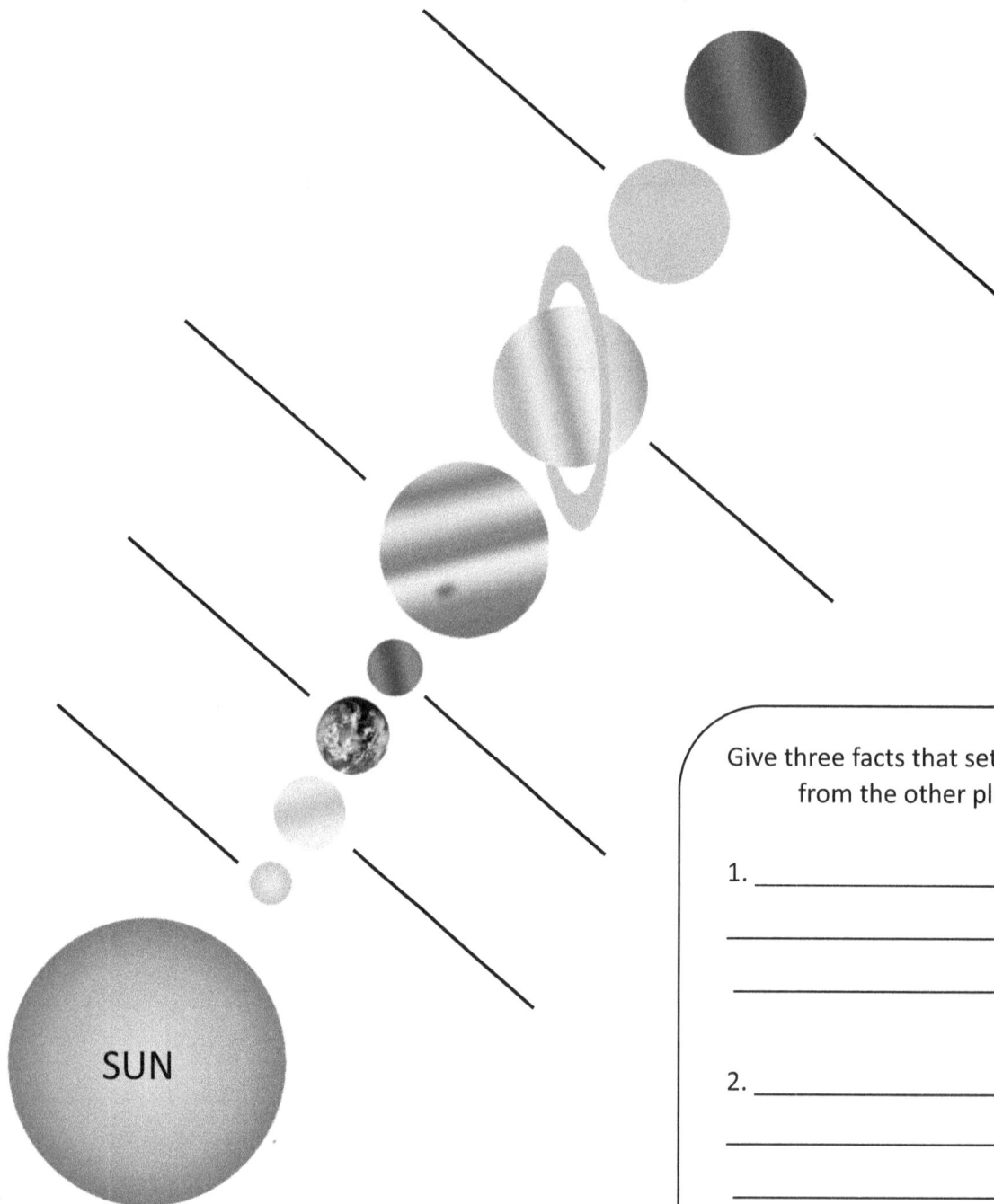

SUN

Give three facts that set **Earth** apart from the other planets.

1. _____

_____

_____

2. _____

_____

_____

3. _____

_____

_____

Layers of the Earth

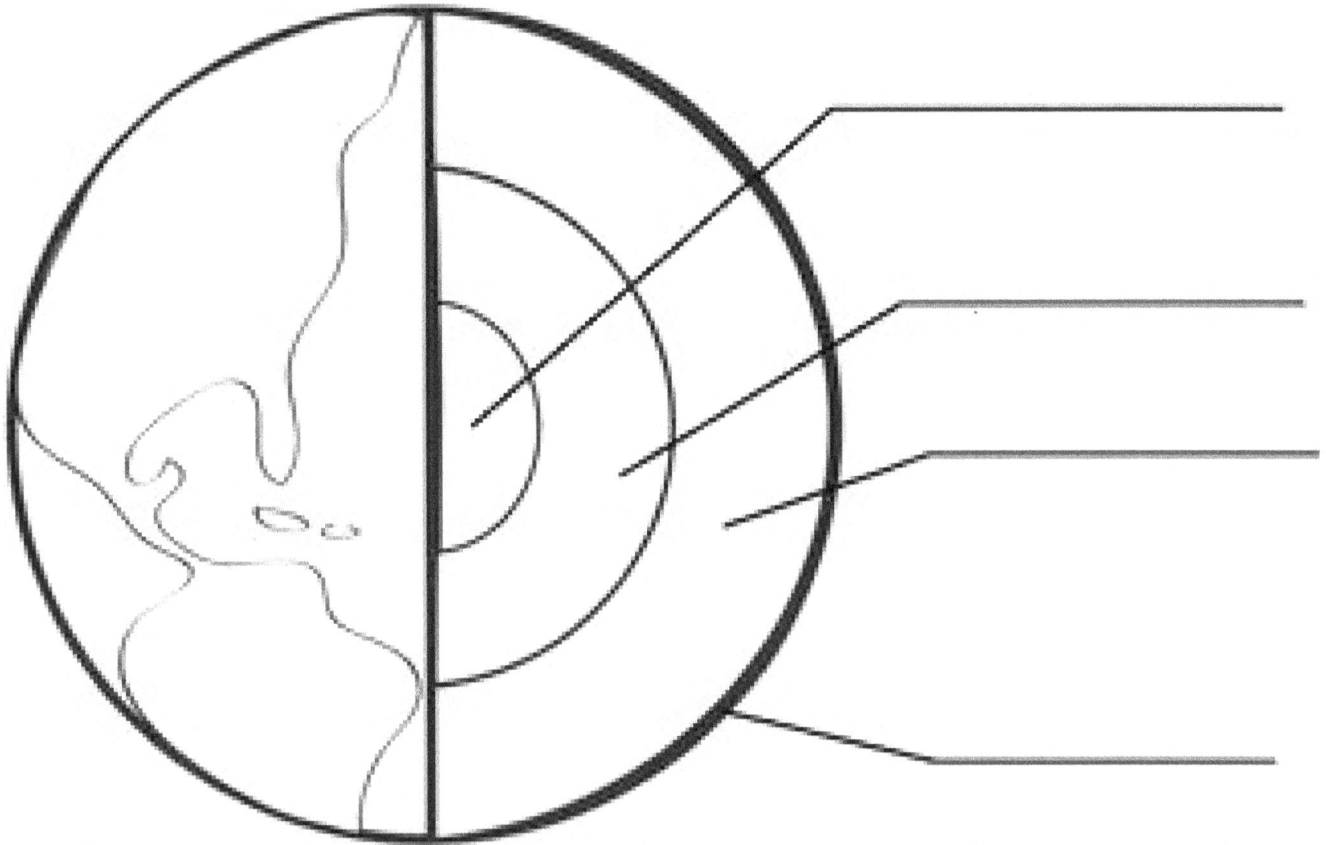

Label the diagram of the Earth above with the following terms. Then fill out the table below giving one fact about each layer.

Crust	Inner Core	Mantle	Outer Core

Layer	Description or fact

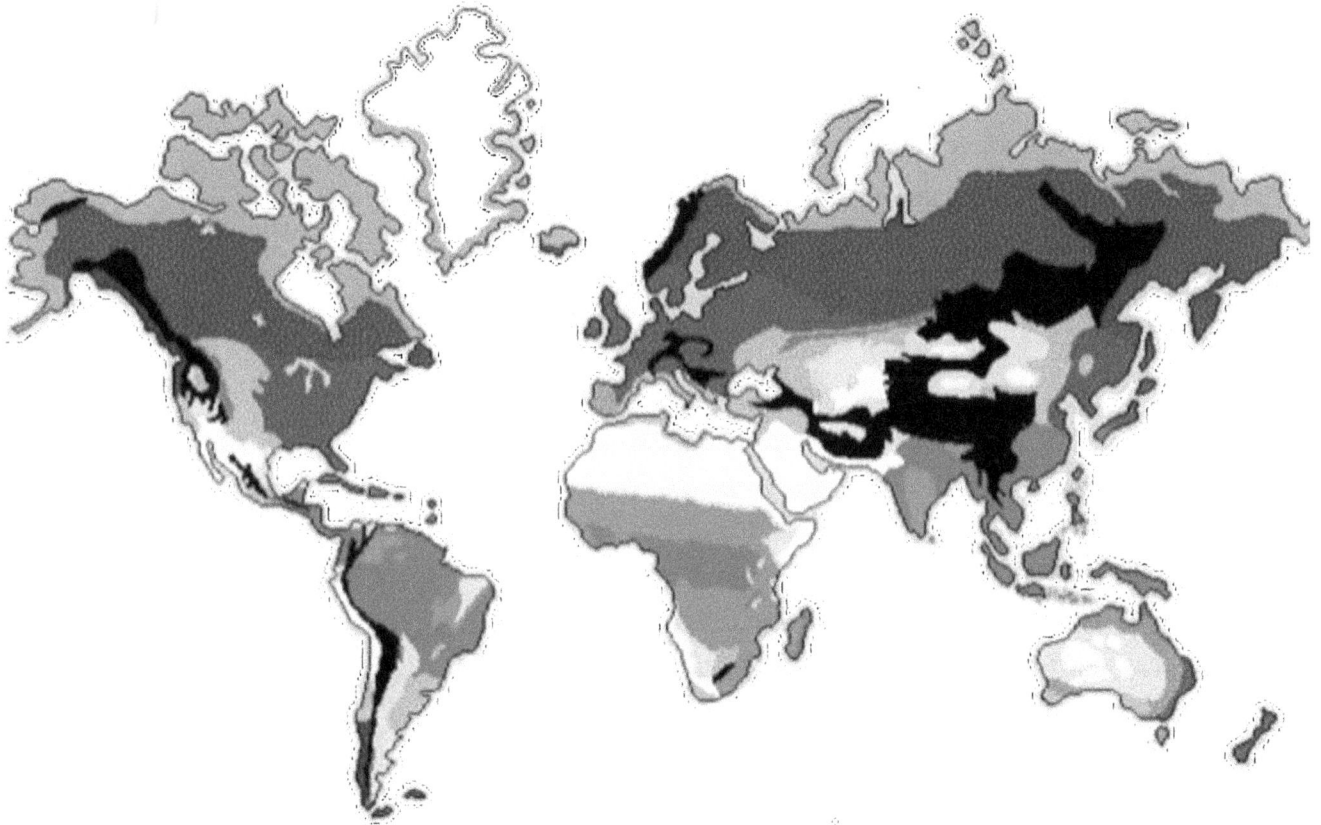

Earth's Biomes

YouTube videos about Earth's Biomes

Rainforest

- Rainforests 101 | National Geographic
  - https://www.youtube.com/watch?v=3vijLre760w

- Creatures of the Amazon Rainforest - National Geographic Documentary
  - https://www.youtube.com/watch?v=qynfHBJ168w

- Rainforest Facts for Kids | All About the Amazon & Other Tropical Rainforests
  - https://www.youtube.com/watch?v=BO4UYhhU-8c

Alpine (Tundra)

- Alpine Tundra Biome Explained
  - https://www.youtube.com/watch?v=_VDP3rYvd04

- Arctic and Alpine Tundra-Tundra Information
  - https://www.youtube.com/watch?v=eXp1sRdQlWY

- Alpine Tundra: Ecogeeks Episode 3
  - https://www.youtube.com/watch?v=xAxtZBh3Zng

Arctic (Tundra)

- Arctic and Alpine Tundra-Tundra Information
  - https://www.youtube.com/watch?v=eXp1sRdQlWY

- Arctic Tundra
  - https://www.youtube.com/watch?v=gUw2N2RbBkM

- Exploring the Arctic for Kids: Arctic Animals and Climates for Children - FreeSchool
  - https://www.youtube.com/watch?v=_kA-_aro3lI

YouTube videos about Earth's Biomes

Taiga (Boreal forest)

- Taiga – Biomes #7
    - https://www.youtube.com/watch?v=OUmHWrF8MnY
- The Taiga-(Boreal Forest)-Biomes of the World
    - https://www.youtube.com/watch?v=gjcs2P9PcMg
- Taiga Biome Facts
    - https://www.youtube.com/watch?v=nLOo4HbLDAs

Desert

- Deserts 101 | National Geographic
    - https://www.youtube.com/watch?v=n4crvs-KTBw
- Desert Animals and Plants | Desert Ecosystem | Desert Video for kids
    - https://www.youtube.com/watch?v=DAs7lqce1cI
- Amazing Ways to Live in the Desert!
    - https://www.youtube.com/watch?v=gaZKEc59g1w

Temperate (Deciduous forest)

- Temperate Forests – Biomes #6
    - https://www.youtube.com/watch?v=K8i0K0pZlCM
- Temperate Climates
    - https://www.youtube.com/watch?v=aaPeDy-ShXo
- Temperate Rainforest of Kenai Fjords National Park
    - https://www.youtube.com/watch?v=rXkvhmgjcqs

YouTube videos about Earth's Biomes

Grassland

- Temperate Grasslands-Biomes of the World
    - https://www.youtube.com/watch?v=I0zeAMkCFpY
- Grasslands - Tropical and Temperate | Social Studies For Grade 5 | Periwinkle
    - https://www.youtube.com/watch?v=k6yVJaWiPcM
- Grasslands – Biomes #5
    - https://www.youtube.com/watch?v=Yy191KVBNP0

Savannah (Tropical grassland)

- Savannah – Biomes #2
    - https://www.youtube.com/watch?v=Mle5gmEpYys
- Savanna Grassland- Biomes of the World
    - https://www.youtube.com/watch?v=k17R7Se28hU
- Savanna Grassland Biome Facts
    - https://www.youtube.com/watch?v=nKnV_7QzpNo

YouTube videos about Earth's Biomes

Marine

- The Marine Biome
  - https://www.youtube.com/watch?v=oQK7IeLJzGI
- Marine Ecosystems
  - https://www.youtube.com/watch?v=EKihcc_AdyA
- Marine Biome
  - https://www.youtube.com/watch?v=g9PIY7RZukk

Freshwater

- Freshwater Biome
  - https://www.youtube.com/watch?v=7qUA9bxqW7g
- Freshwater Biomes
  - https://www.youtube.com/watch?v=txjTUP4_msk
- Types of Freshwater Ecosystems-Lakes-Ponds-River-Streams-Wetlands
  - https://www.youtube.com/watch?v=SexLZIyo_FA

Earth's Biomes - Rainforest

Color the areas on the map where you can find the **Rainforest** Biome.

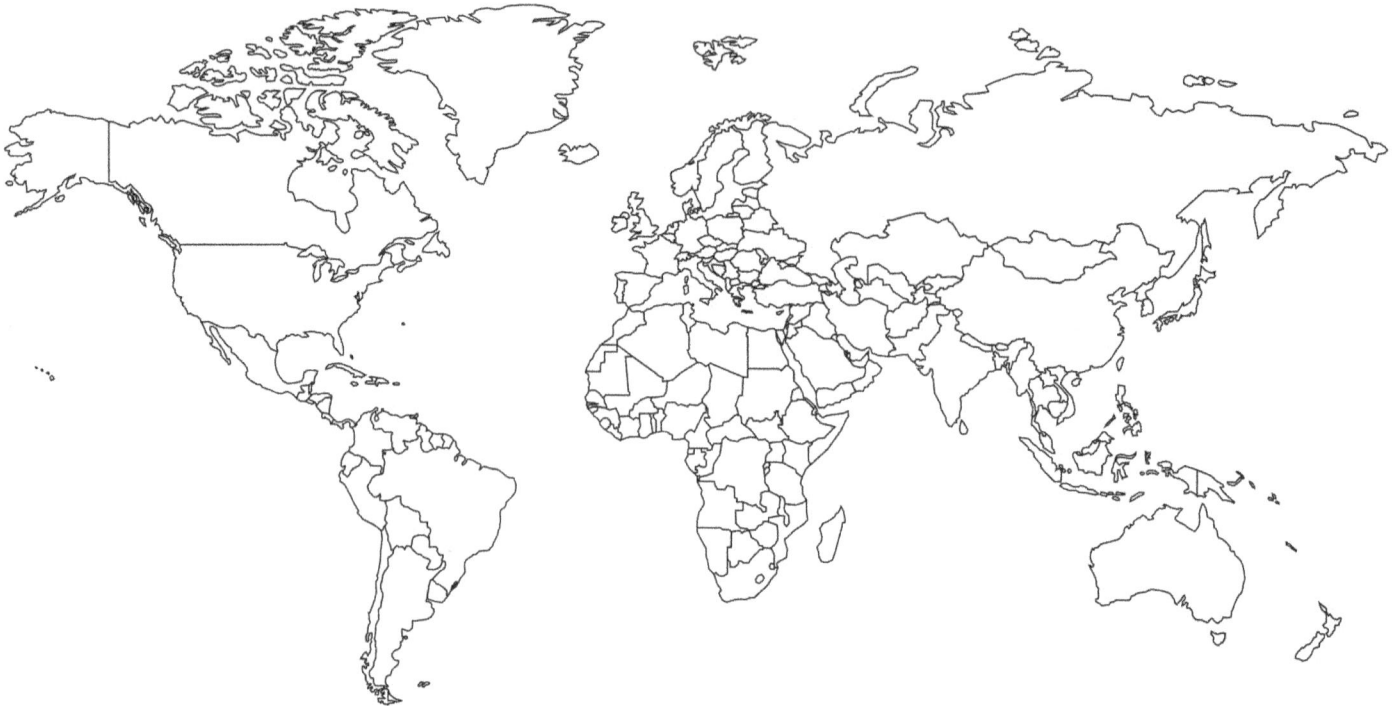

This biome is (circle one):	Terrestrial	Aquatic

Write a description of this land and climate of biome:

Name 3 types of **plants** native to this biome:

Name 3 types of **animals** native to this biome:

Animals of The Rainforest Biome

Fill out the following boxes with animals that are native to **the Rainforest Biome**

Animal Common Name

_____

Scientific Name

_____

List 3 facts about this animal

1. _____

   _____

2. _____

   _____

3. _____

   _____

Animal Common Name

_____

Scientific Name

_____

List 3 facts about this animal

1. _____

   _____

2. _____

   _____

3. _____

   _____

Animal Common Name

_____

Scientific Name

_____

List 3 facts about this animal

1. _____

   _____

2. _____

   _____

3. _____

   _____

Animal Common Name

_____

Scientific Name

_____

List 3 facts about this animal

1. _____

   _____

2. _____

   _____

3. _____

   _____

Earth's Biomes – Alpine (Tundra)

Color the areas on the map where you can find the **Alpine** Biome.

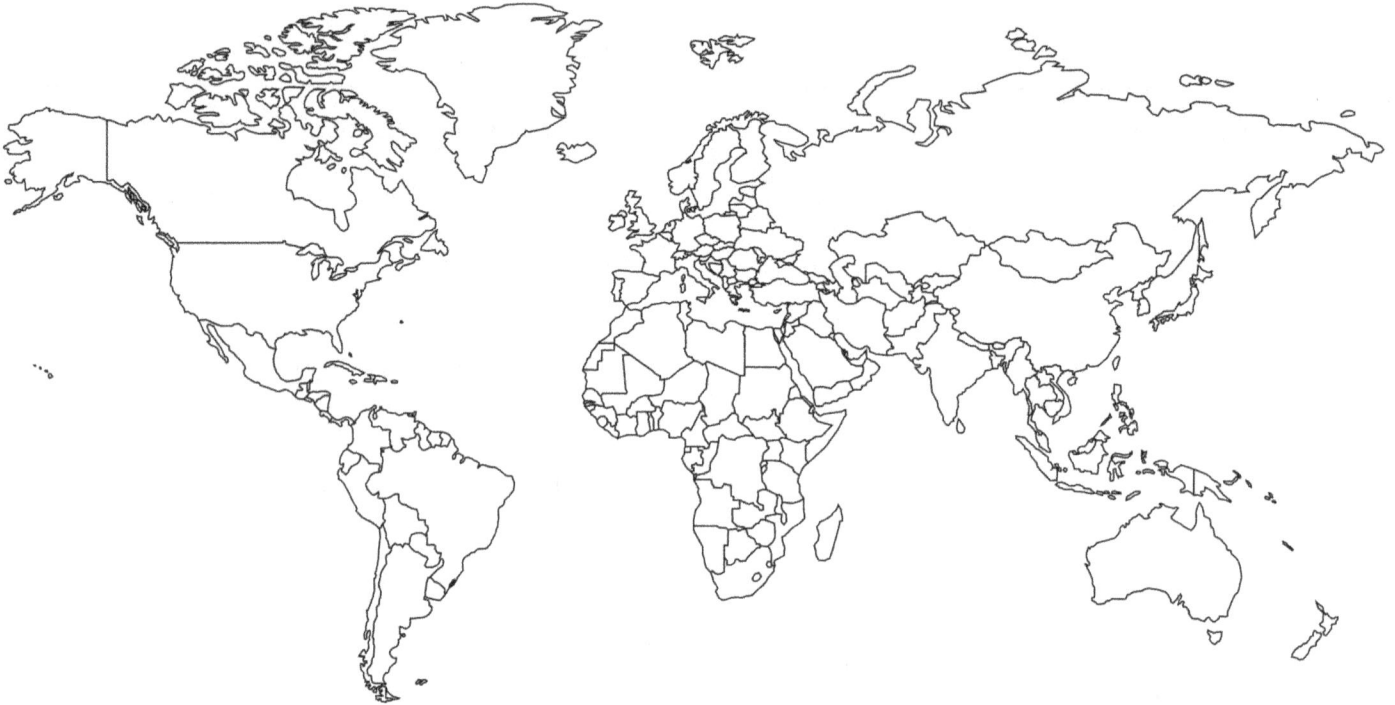

This biome is (circle one):	Terrestrial	Aquatic

Write a description of this land and climate of biome:

Name 3 types of **plants** native to this biome:

Name 3 types of **animals** native to this biome:

Animals of The Alpine Biome

Fill out the following boxes with animals that are native to **the Alpine Biome**

Animal Common Name

_____

Scientific Name

_____

List 3 facts about this animal

1. _____

   _____

2. _____

   _____

3. _____

   _____

Animal Common Name

_____

Scientific Name

_____

List 3 facts about this animal

1. _____

   _____

2. _____

   _____

3. _____

   _____

Animal Common Name

_____

Scientific Name

_____

List 3 facts about this animal

1. _____

   _____

2. _____

   _____

3. _____

   _____

Animal Common Name

_____

Scientific Name

_____

List 3 facts about this animal

1. _____

   _____

2. _____

   _____

3. _____

   _____

Earth's Biomes – Arctic (Tundra)

Color the areas on the map where you can find the **Arctic** Biome.

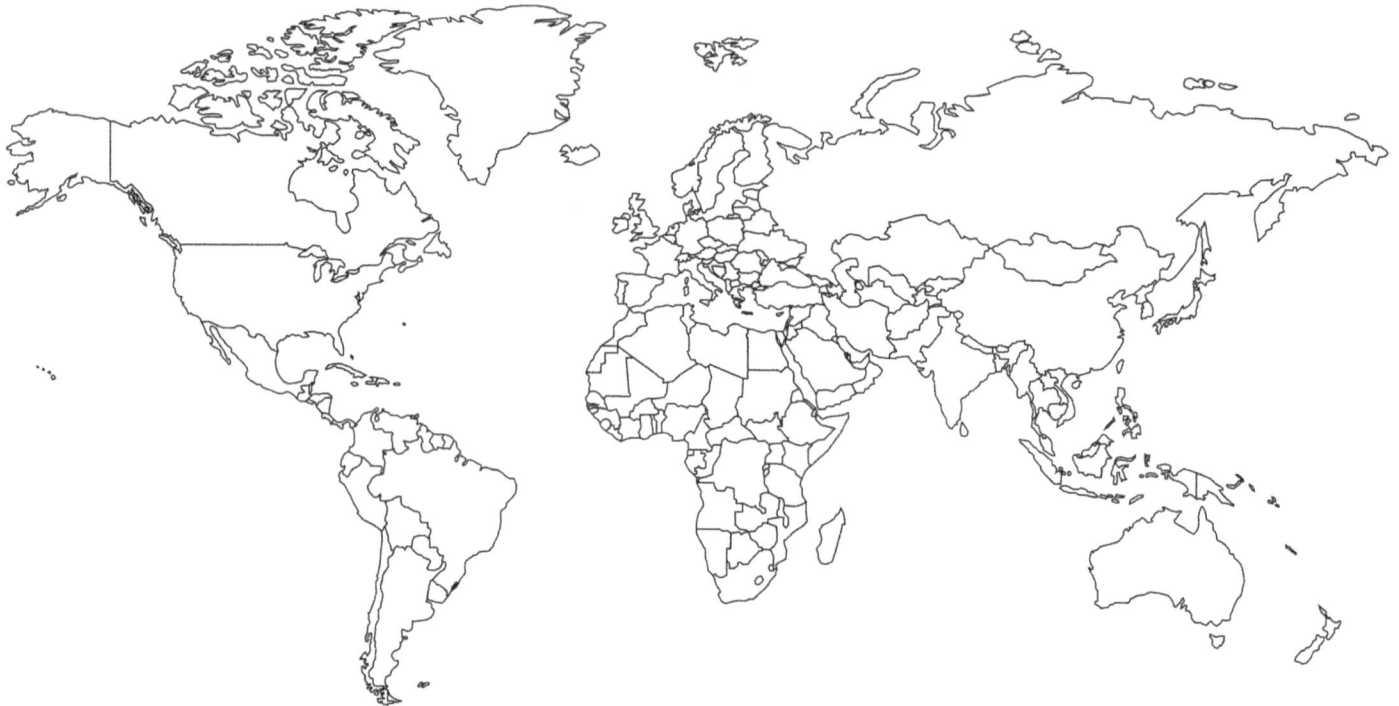

This biome is (circle one):	Terrestrial	Aquatic

Write a description of this land and climate of biome:

Name 3 types of **plants** native to this biome:

Name 3 types of **animals** native to this biome:

Animals of The Arctic Biome

Fill out the following boxes with animals that are native to **the Arctic Biome**

Animal Common Name

_____

Scientific Name

_____

List 3 facts about this animal

1. _____

   _____

2. _____

   _____

3. _____

   _____

Animal Common Name

_____

Scientific Name

_____

List 3 facts about this animal

1. _____

   _____

2. _____

   _____

3. _____

   _____

Animal Common Name

_____

Scientific Name

_____

List 3 facts about this animal

1. _____

   _____

2. _____

   _____

3. _____

   _____

Animal Common Name

_____

Scientific Name

_____

List 3 facts about this animal

1. _____

   _____

2. _____

   _____

3. _____

   _____

Earth's Biomes – Taiga (Boreal Forest)

Color the areas on the map where you can find the **Taiga** Biome.

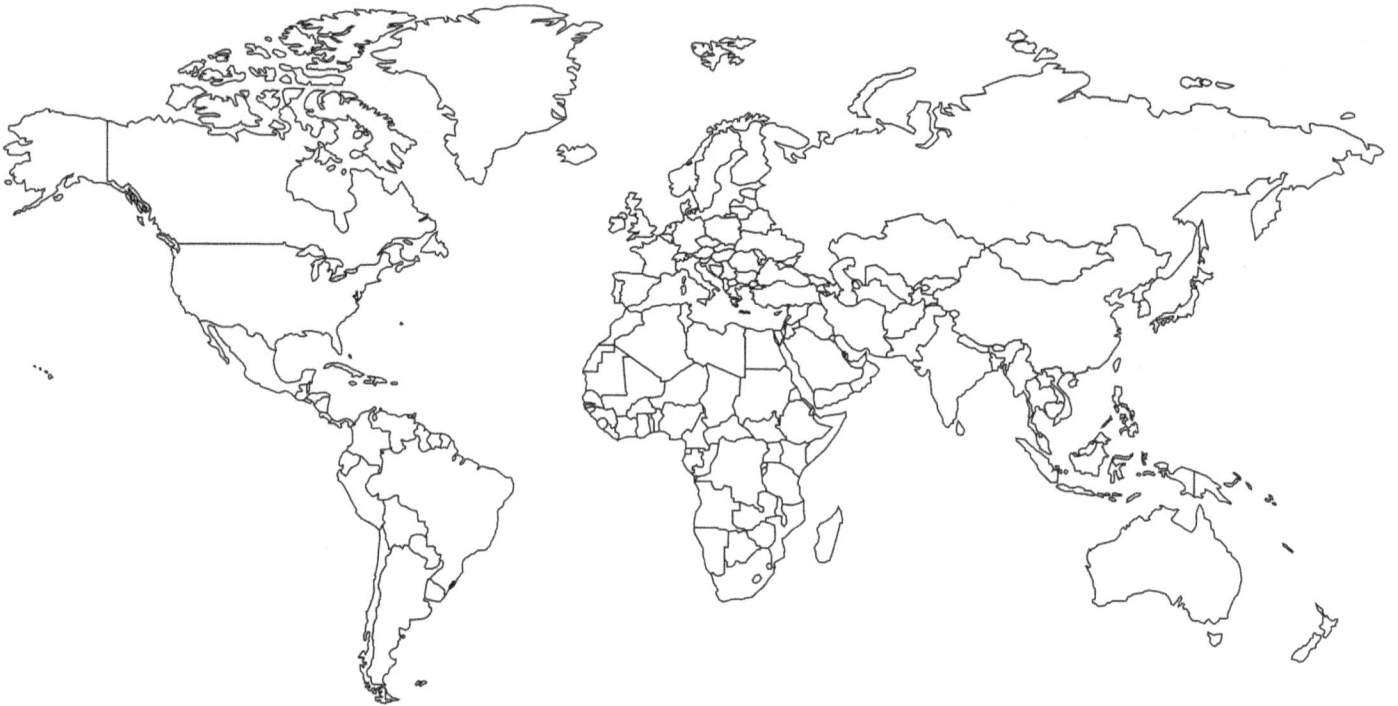

This biome is (circle one):	Terrestrial	Aquatic

Write a description of this land and climate of biome:

Name 3 types of **plants** native to this biome:

Name 3 types of **animals** native to this biome:

Animals of The Taiga Biome

Fill out the following boxes with animals that are native to **the Taiga Biome**

Animal Common Name

_____

Scientific Name

_____

List 3 facts about this animal

1. _____
   _____
2. _____
   _____
3. _____
   _____

Animal Common Name

_____

Scientific Name

_____

List 3 facts about this animal

1. _____
   _____
2. _____
   _____
3. _____
   _____

Animal Common Name

_____

Scientific Name

_____

List 3 facts about this animal

1. _____
   _____
2. _____
   _____
3. _____
   _____

Animal Common Name

_____

Scientific Name

_____

List 3 facts about this animal

1. _____
   _____
2. _____
   _____
3. _____
   _____

Earth's Biomes - Desert

Color the areas on the map where you can find the **Desert** Biome.

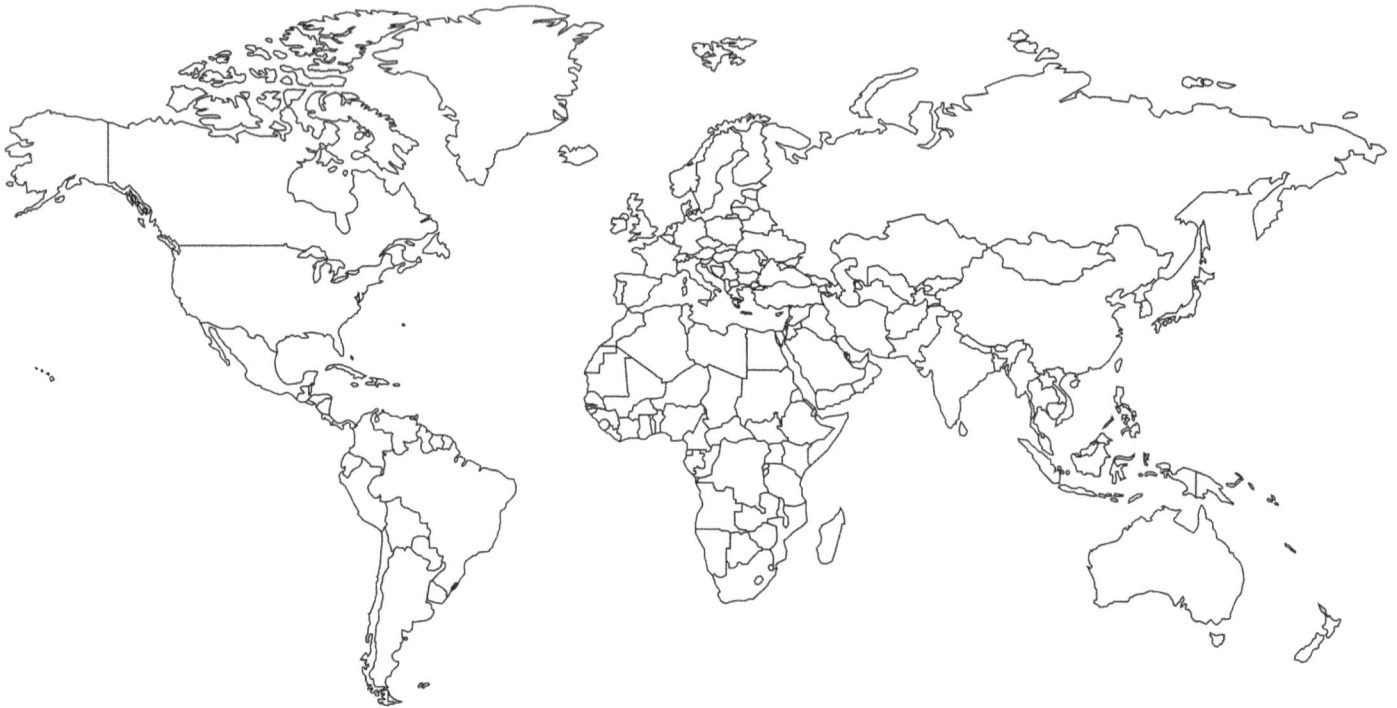

This biome is (circle one):	Terrestrial	Aquatic

Write a description of this land and climate of biome:

Name 3 types of **plants** native to this biome:

Name 3 types of **animals** native to this biome:

Animals of The Desert Biome

Fill out the following boxes with animals that are native to **the Desert Biome**

Animal Common Name

_____

Scientific Name

_____

List 3 facts about this animal

1. _____

   _____

2. _____

   _____

3. _____

   _____

Animal Common Name

_____

Scientific Name

_____

List 3 facts about this animal

1. _____

   _____

2. _____

   _____

3. _____

   _____

Animal Common Name

_____

Scientific Name

_____

List 3 facts about this animal

1. _____

   _____

2. _____

   _____

3. _____

   _____

Animal Common Name

_____

Scientific Name

_____

List 3 facts about this animal

1. _____

   _____

2. _____

   _____

3. _____

   _____

Earth's Biomes – Temperate (Deciduous Forest)

Color the areas on the map where you can find the **Temperate** Biome.

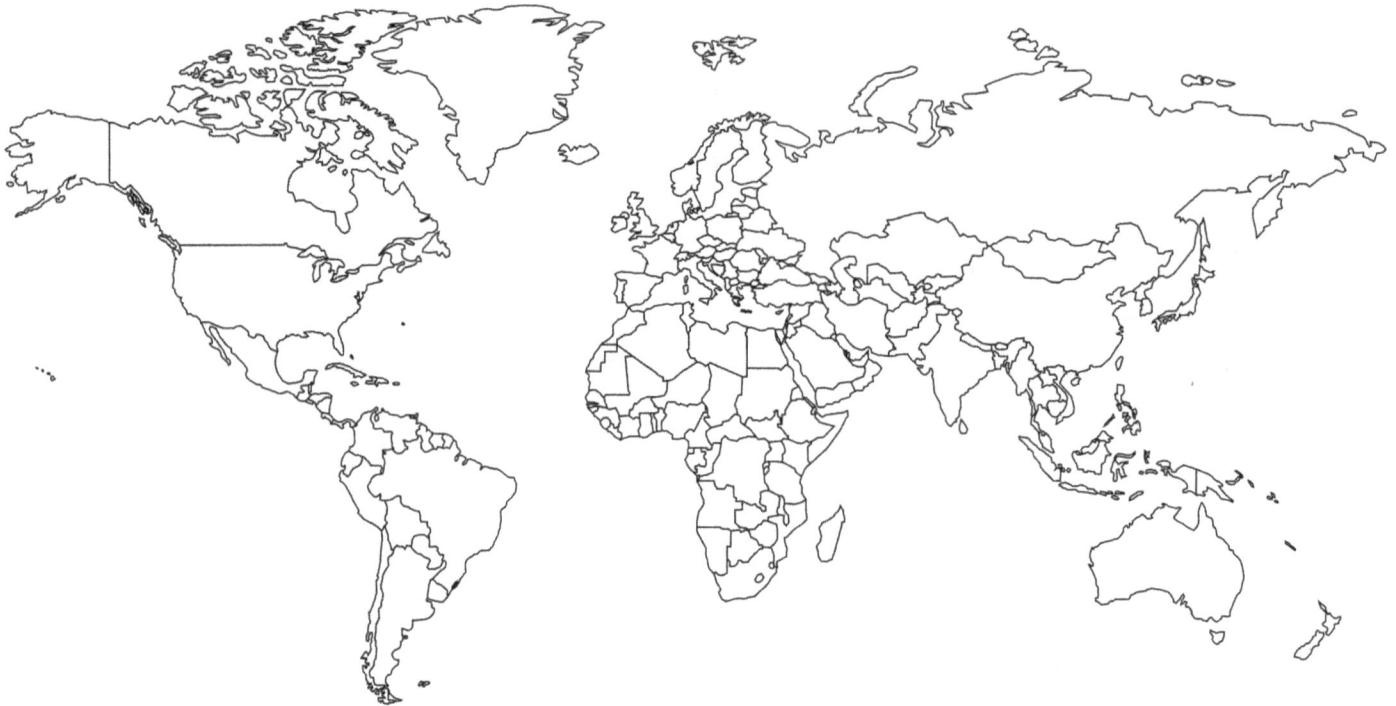

This biome is (circle one):	Terrestrial	Aquatic

Write a description of this land and climate of biome:

Name 3 types of **plants** native to this biome:

Name 3 types of **animals** native to this biome:

Animals of The Temperate Biome

Fill out the following boxes with animals that are native to **the Temperate Biome**

Animal Common Name

_____

Scientific Name

_____

List 3 facts about this animal

1. _____

   _____

2. _____

   _____

3. _____

   _____

Animal Common Name

_____

Scientific Name

_____

List 3 facts about this animal

1. _____

   _____

2. _____

   _____

3. _____

   _____

Animal Common Name

_____

Scientific Name

_____

List 3 facts about this animal

1. _____

   _____

2. _____

   _____

3. _____

   _____

Animal Common Name

_____

Scientific Name

_____

List 3 facts about this animal

1. _____

   _____

2. _____

   _____

3. _____

   _____

Earth's Biomes - Grassland

Color the areas on the map where you can find the **Grasslands** Biome.

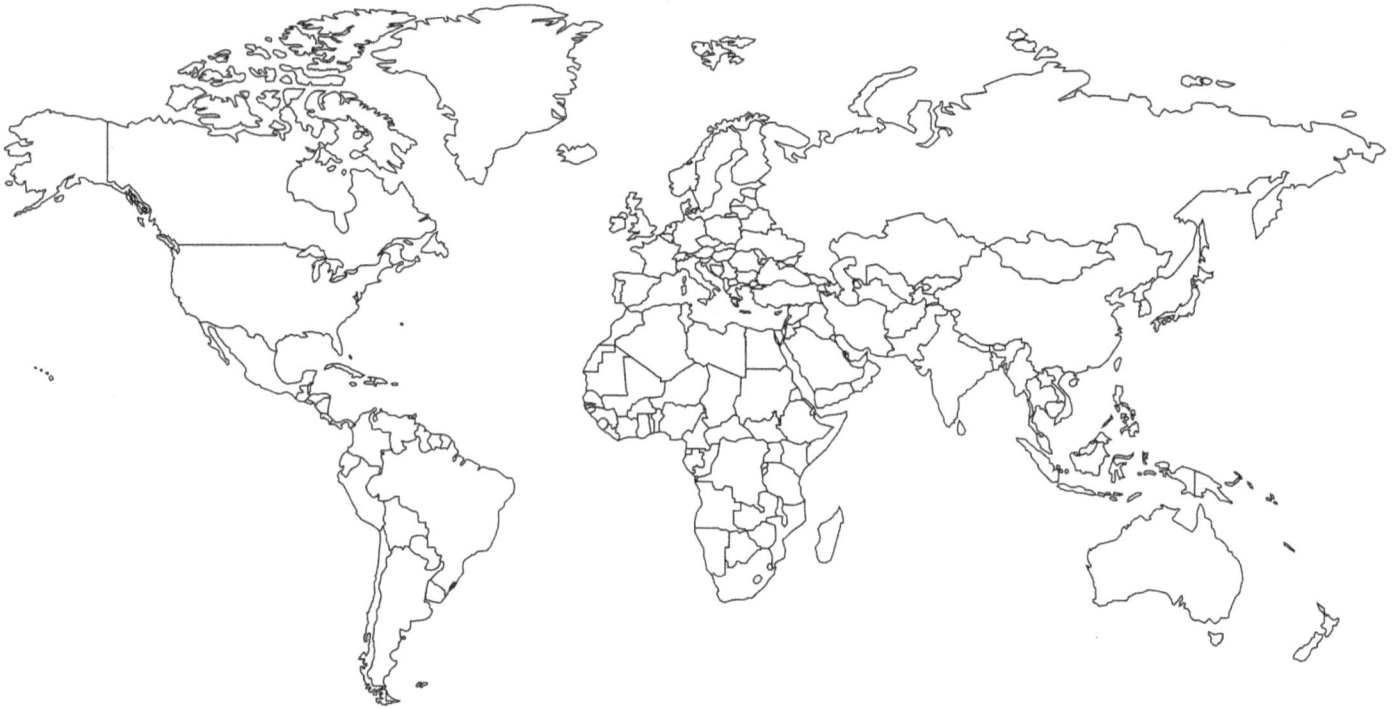

This biome is (circle one):	Terrestrial	Aquatic

Write a description of this land and climate of biome:

Name 3 types of **plants** native to this biome:

Name 3 types of **animals** native to this biome:

Animals of The Grassland Biome

Fill out the following boxes with animals that are native to **the Grassland Biome**

Animal Common Name

_____

Scientific Name

_____

List 3 facts about this animal

1. _____

_____

2. _____

_____

3. _____

_____

Animal Common Name

_____

Scientific Name

_____

List 3 facts about this animal

1. _____

_____

2. _____

_____

3. _____

_____

Animal Common Name

_____

Scientific Name

_____

List 3 facts about this animal

1. _____

_____

2. _____

_____

3. _____

_____

Animal Common Name

_____

Scientific Name

_____

List 3 facts about this animal

1. _____

_____

2. _____

_____

3. _____

_____

Earth's Biomes – Savannah (Tropical Grassland)

Color the areas on the map where you can find the **Savannah** Biome.

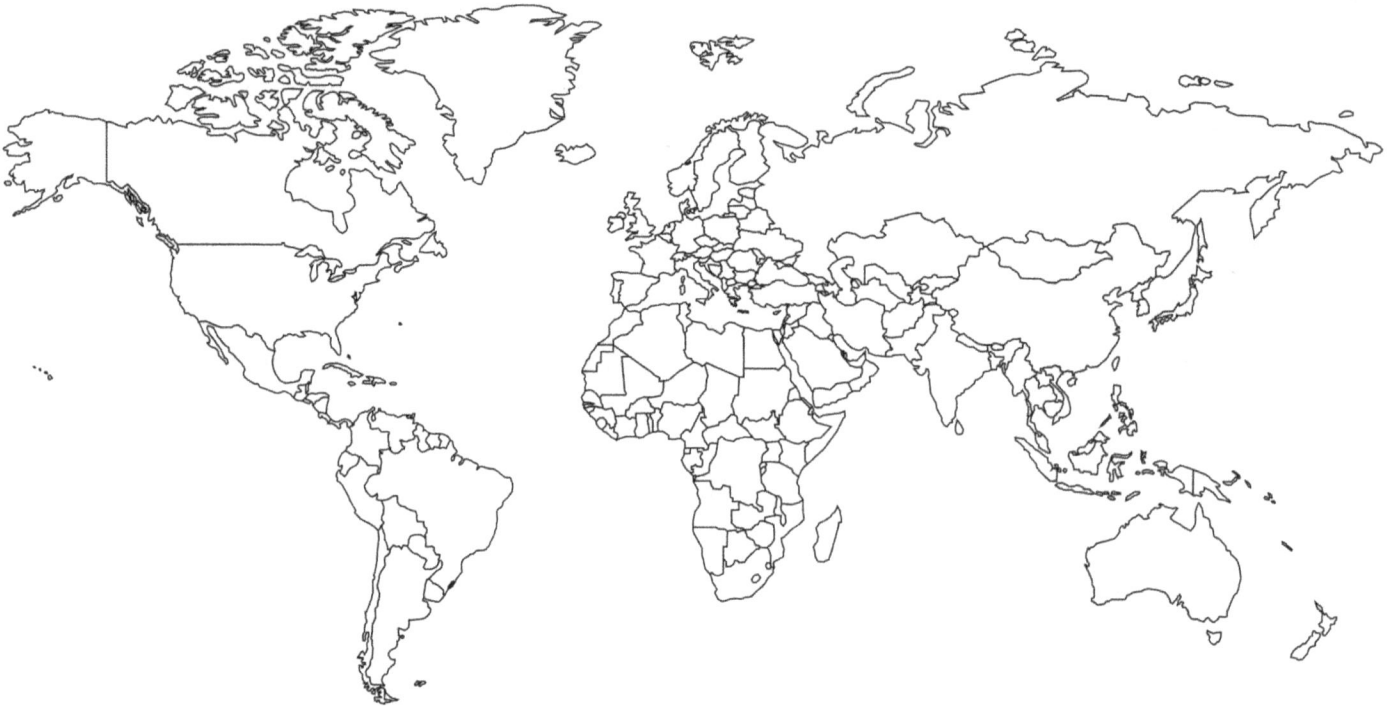

This biome is (circle one):	Terrestrial	Aquatic

Write a description of this land and climate of biome:

Name 3 types of **plants** native to this biome:

Name 3 types of **animals** native to this biome:

Animals of The Savannah Biome

Fill out the following boxes with animals that are native to **the Savannah Biome**

Animal Common Name
_____

Scientific Name
_____

List 3 facts about this animal
1. _____
_____
2. _____
_____
3. _____
_____

Animal Common Name
_____

Scientific Name
_____

List 3 facts about this animal
1. _____
_____
2. _____
_____
3. _____
_____

Animal Common Name
_____

Scientific Name
_____

List 3 facts about this animal
1. _____
_____
2. _____
_____
3. _____
_____

Animal Common Name
_____

Scientific Name
_____

List 3 facts about this animal
1. _____
_____
2. _____
_____
3. _____
_____

Earth's Biomes - Marine

Color the areas on the map where you can find the **Marine** Biome.

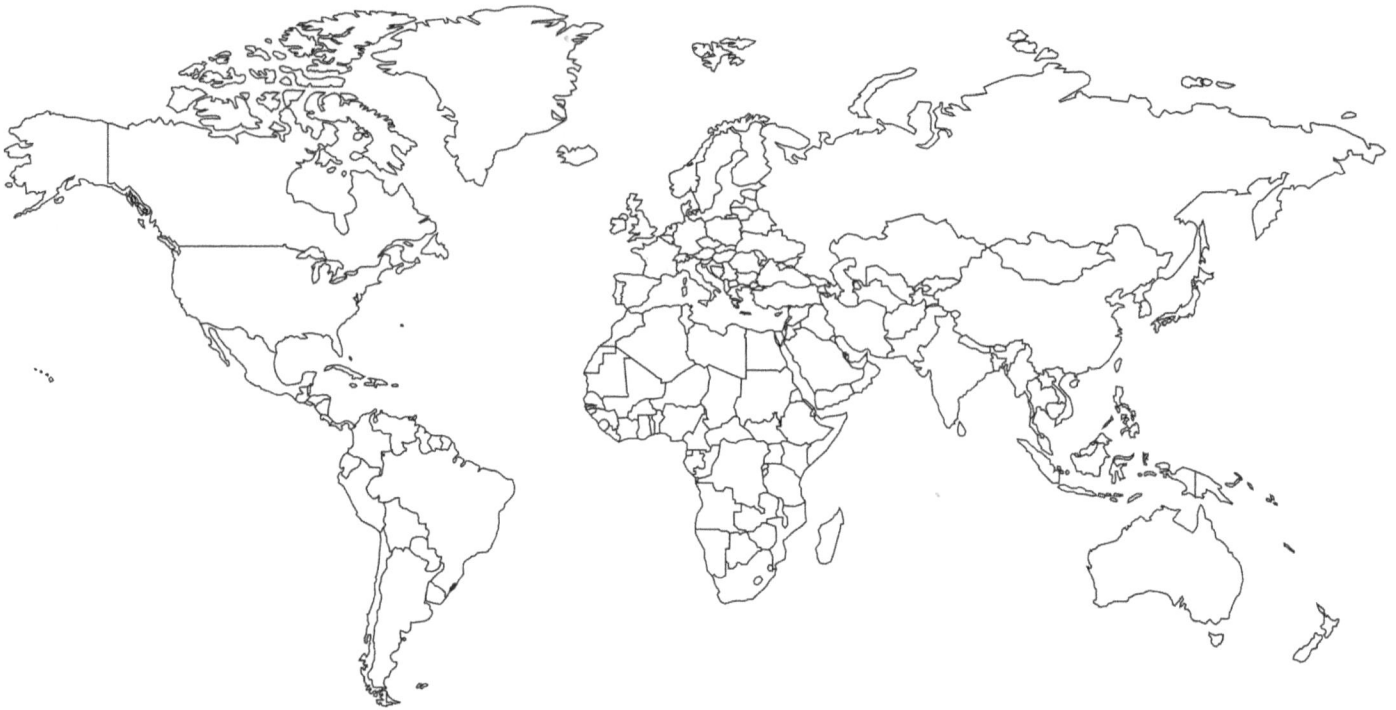

This biome is (circle one):	Terrestrial	Aquatic

Write a description of this land and climate of biome:

Name 3 types of **plants** native to this biome:

Name 3 types of **animals** native to this biome:

Animals of The Marine Biome

Fill out the following boxes with animals that are native to **the Marine Biome**

Animal Common Name

_____

Scientific Name

_____

List 3 facts about this animal

1. _____
   _____
2. _____
   _____
3. _____
   _____

Animal Common Name

_____

Scientific Name

_____

List 3 facts about this animal

1. _____
   _____
2. _____
   _____
3. _____
   _____

Animal Common Name

_____

Scientific Name

_____

List 3 facts about this animal

1. _____
   _____
2. _____
   _____
3. _____
   _____

Animal Common Name

_____

Scientific Name

_____

List 3 facts about this animal

1. _____
   _____
2. _____
   _____
3. _____
   _____

Earth's Biomes - Freshwater

Color the areas on the map where you can find the **Freshwater** Biome.

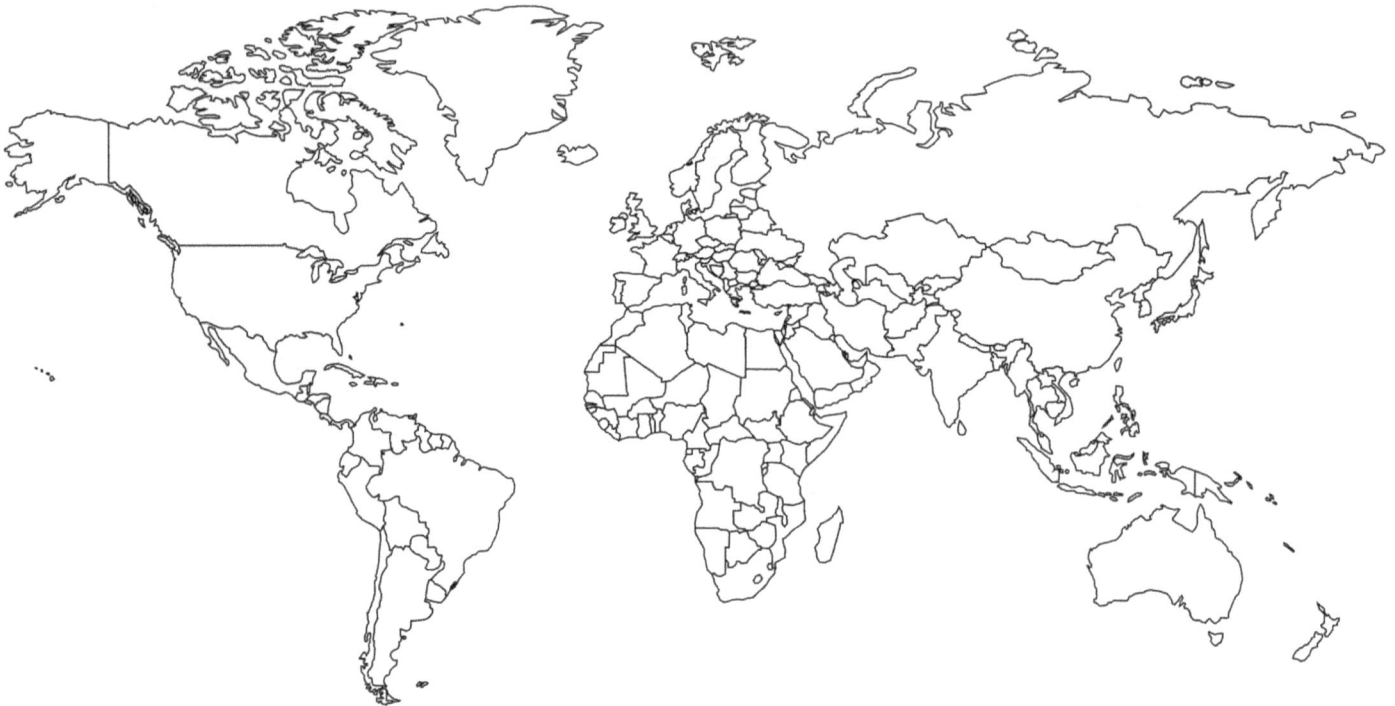

This biome is (circle one):	Terrestrial	Aquatic

Write a description of this land and climate of biome:

Name 3 types of **plants** native to this biome:

Name 3 types of **animals** native to this biome:

Animals of The Freshwater Biome

Fill out the following boxes with animals that are native to **the Freshwater Biome**

Animal Common Name

_____

Scientific Name

_____

List 3 facts about this animal

1. _____

   _____

2. _____

   _____

3. _____

   _____

Animal Common Name

_____

Scientific Name

_____

List 3 facts about this animal

1. _____

   _____

2. _____

   _____

3. _____

   _____

Animal Common Name

_____

Scientific Name

_____

List 3 facts about this animal

1. _____

   _____

2. _____

   _____

3. _____

   _____

Animal Common Name

_____

Scientific Name

_____

List 3 facts about this animal

1. _____

   _____

2. _____

   _____

3. _____

   _____

Alpine vs Arctic

Complete the Venn Diagram comparing Alpine to Arctic biomes.

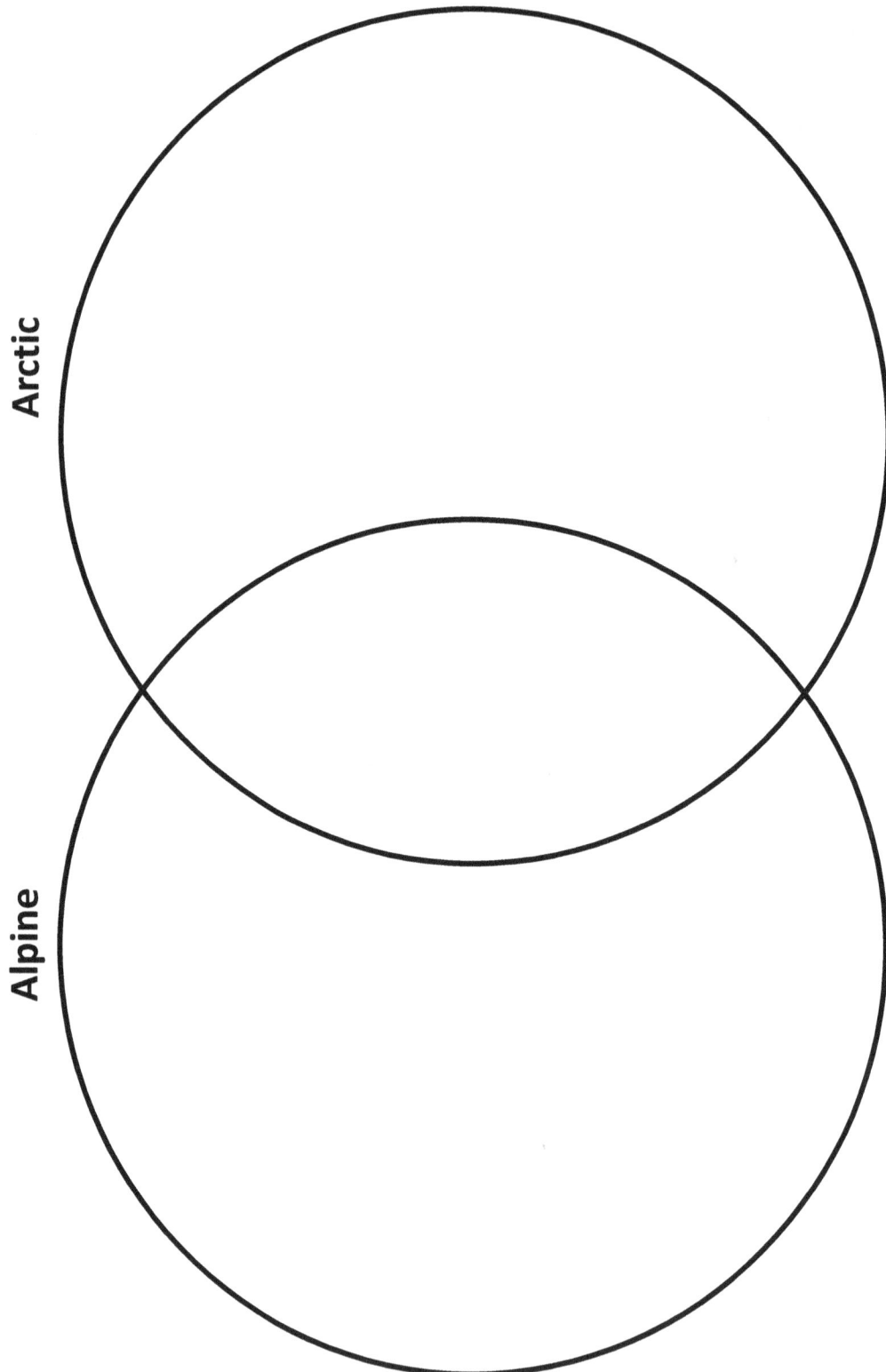

Arctic

Alpine

Grassland vs Savannah

Complete the Venn Diagram comparing Grassland to Savannah biomes.

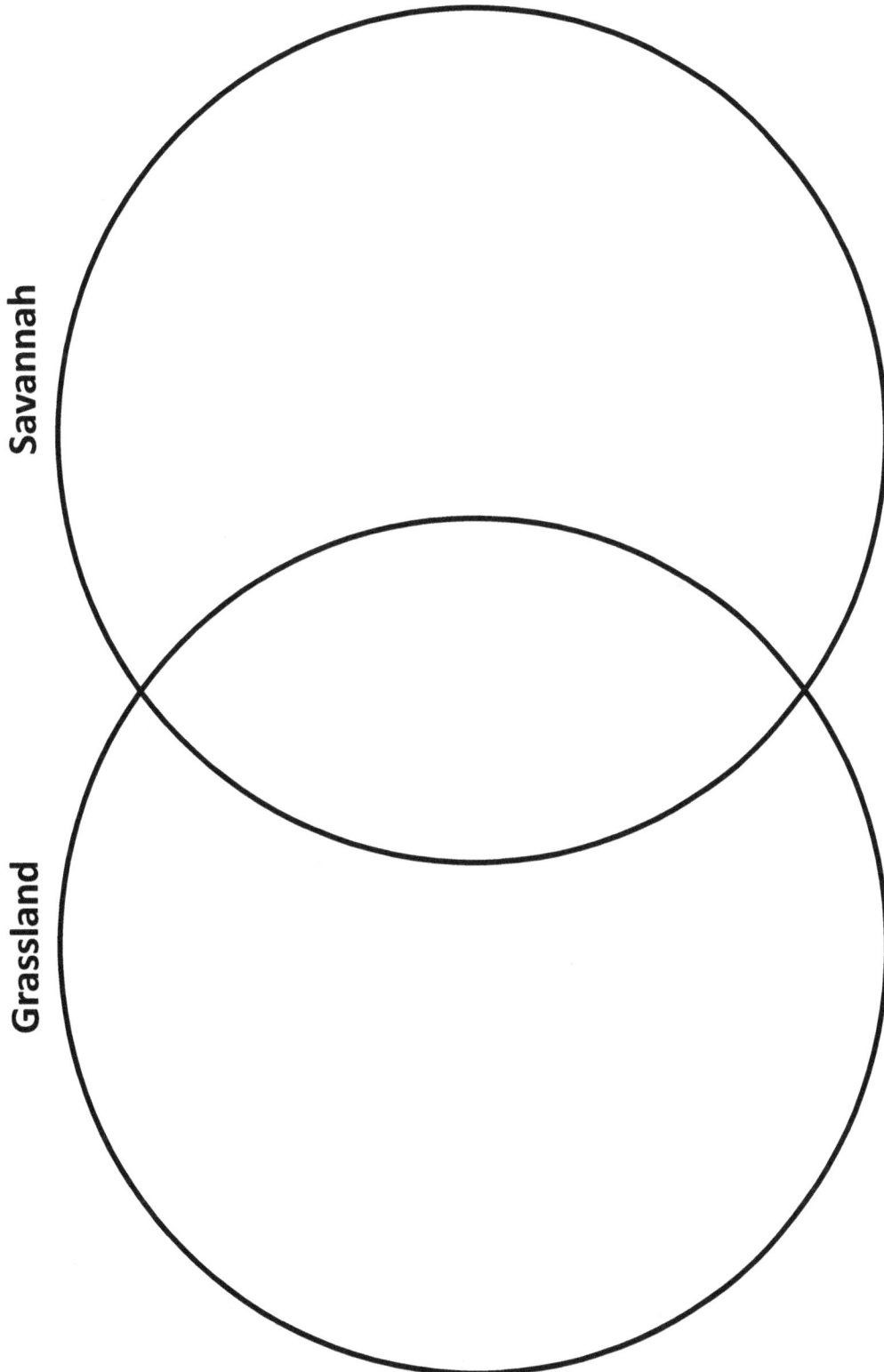

Savannah

Grassland

Fresh Water vs Marine

Complete the Venn Diagram comparing Fresh water to Marine biomes.

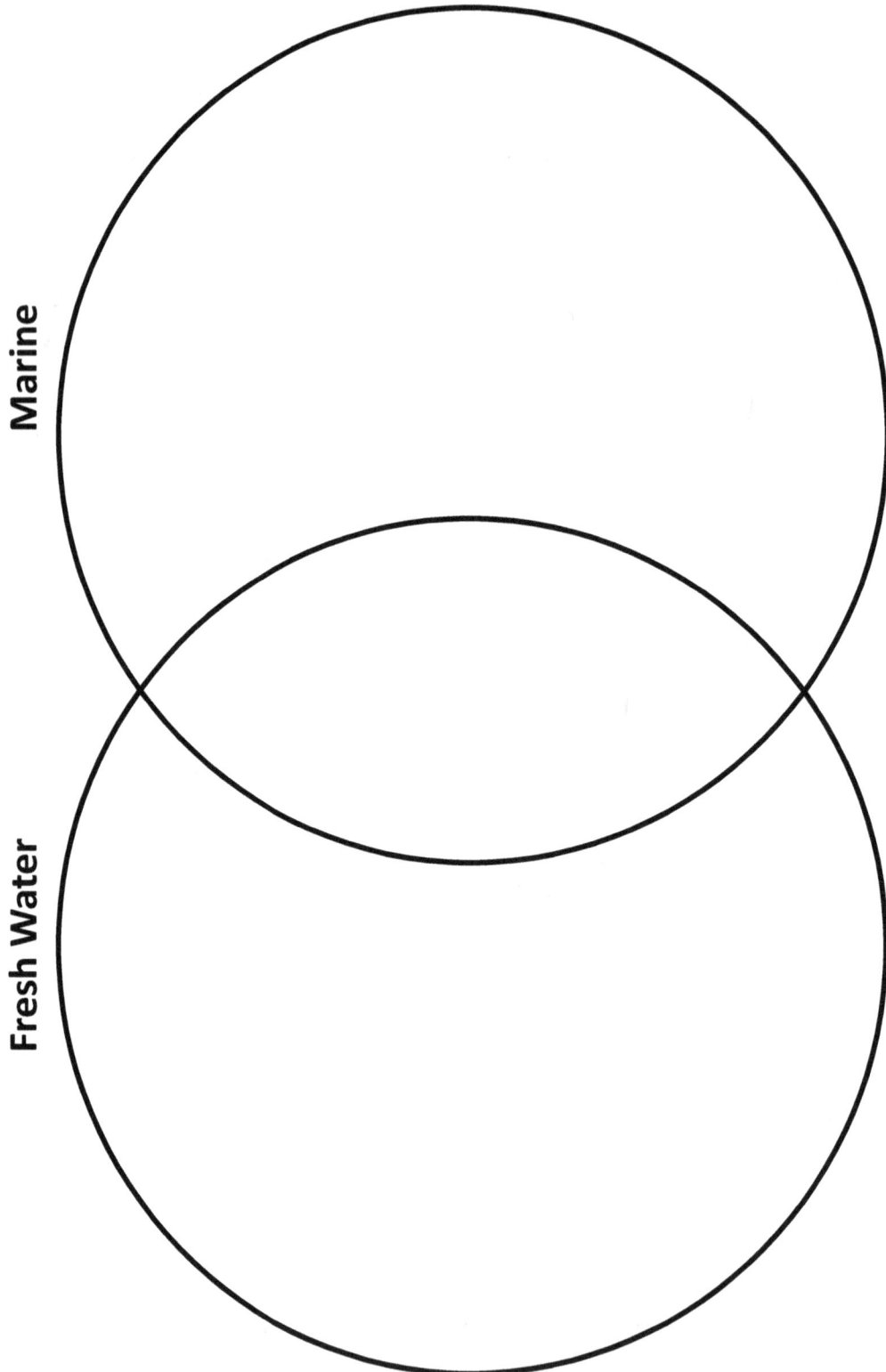

Marine

Fresh Water

The Oceans

Books about the Oceans

1. (Y) *The Magic Schoolbus: On the Ocean Floor* by Joanna Cole

2. (Y) *Shark Lady* by Jess Keating

3. (Y) *Save the Ocean* by Bethany Stahl

4. (Y) *The Brilliant Deep* by Kate Messner

5. (Y) *I Love you Oceanly* by Lynn Sutton

6. (O) *Into the Planet: My Life as a Cave Diver* by Jill Heinerth

7. (O) *Oceanology: The Secrets of the Sea Revealed* by DK

8. (O) *The Sea Around Us* by Rachel Carson

9. (Y) *Ocean Anatomy: The Curious Parts & Pieces of the World under the Sea* by Julia Rothman

10. (O) *Expedition Deep Ocean: The First Descent to the Bottom of All Five Oceans* by Josh Young

* (O) books are for older readers; (Y) books are for younger readers

Games about Oceans

1. North Star Games Oceans Board Game

2. Go Fish

3. Ocean Labyrinth

4. Oceanopoly

5. Ocean Bingo Game

6. Don't Rock the Boat

7. Outset Media Prof. Noggin-Life in The Ocean

8. LogicRoots Ocean Raiders Math Addition Board Game

9. Outset Media Board Games - Ocean Picture Dominoes

10. Reef Board Game

Movies about the Oceans

1. Oceans (G)(2009)

2. Mission Blue (NR)(2014)

3. Chasing Coral (2017)

4. Finding Nemo (G) (2003)

5. Turtle: The Incredible Journey (2009)

6. 20,000 Leagues Under The Sea (1954)

7. Atlantis: The Lost Empire (2001)

8. Aquaman (2018)

9. The Little Mermaid (1989)

10. Big Miracle (2012)

YouTube videos about the Oceans

General Ocean Videos

- Blue Planet: The Fascinating World Beneath the Waves | Free Documentary Nature
  - https://www.youtube.com/watch?v=CnmLgezy3jc

- Our Planet | High Seas | FULL EPISODE | Netflix
  - https://www.youtube.com/watch?v=9FqwhW0B3tY

- Deep Beneath The Ocean and Its Mysterious Creatures - Full Documentary HD
  - https://www.youtube.com/watch?v=zZMguwlkdPY

Pacific Ocean

- Big Pacific. E1 (Nature Documentary)
  - https://www.youtube.com/watch?v=dgIUsmP5KTo

- The Pacific Ocean is VASTLY Bigger Than You Think
  - https://www.youtube.com/watch?v=3DZmXYl3xVE&pbjreload=101

- The Great Pacific Garbage Patch
  - https://www.youtube.com/watch?v=MnCbTTTi7ic

- Why the Atlantic and Pacific Oceans Don't Mix
  - https://www.youtube.com/watch?v=U93QRMcQU5Y

Atlantic Ocean

- Middle of the Atlantic Ocean
  - https://www.youtube.com/watch?v=THfL_OI1gt4

- The Sea Monsters of Atlantic - (Best Sea-life Documentary)
  - https://www.youtube.com/watch?v=H7TEY2A5bs0

- What Happened To Atlantis?
  - https://www.youtube.com/watch?v=_iih05QEvoM

- How the Atlantic Ocean Got its Name
  - https://www.youtube.com/watch?v=kN88RP3XWUU

YouTube videos about the Oceans

Indian Ocean

- 10 facts about the Indian Ocean
    - https://www.youtube.com/watch?v=gYnO4QjfUYc
- Global Reef Expedition: Indian Ocean
    - https://www.youtube.com/watch?v=VfZ0PEe4c8U
- Int'l Commerce, Snorkeling Camels, and The Indian Ocean Trade: Crash Course World History #18
    - https://www.youtube.com/watch?v=a6XtBLDmPA0
- Descent into the Indian Ocean
    - https://www.youtube.com/watch?v=y4sQxBfoVc4

Arctic Ocean

- Arctic | Exploring Oceans
    - https://www.youtube.com/watch?v=umAeFKF2uxA
- TOP 15 Facts About The Arctic Ocean
    - https://www.youtube.com/watch?v=zjLs88MqCB8
- Who Owns The Arctic Ocean?
    - https://www.youtube.com/watch?v=pk9Z7xrRCRY

Southern Ocean

- The Southern Ocean
    - https://www.youtube.com/watch?v=ARjobIyDKCA
- Interesting Southern Ocean Facts
    - https://www.youtube.com/watch?v=XXhvVl8qe-0
- SOCCOM: Understanding the Southern Ocean
    - https://www.youtube.com/watch?v=682x1Zw4SpQ

Layers of the Ocean

Label the diagram of the Ocean above with the following terms. Then fill out the table below giving one fact about each layer.

Sunlit Zone	Trenches	Dark Zone	Abyss	Twilight Zone

Layer	Description or fact

Ocean Fact File: Atlantic

Color the location of the Atlantic Ocean on the Map.

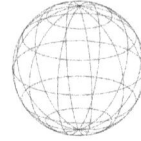

Hemisphere (circle one)

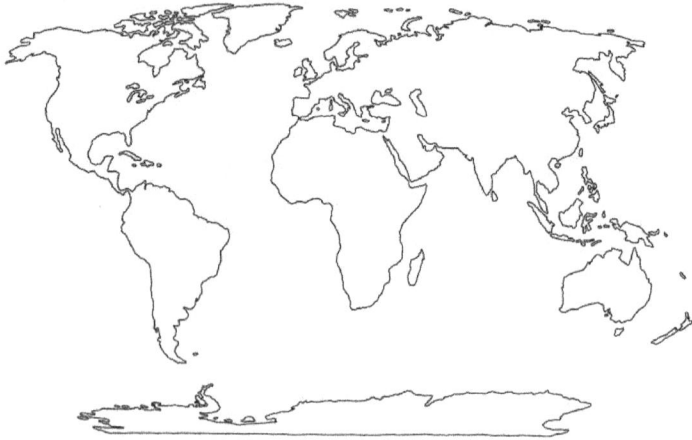

Northern

Southern

Both

FACTS

Maximum Depth:_____

Location of Deepest Point: _____

Warmest Temperature: _____

Coldest Temperature: _____

Other Cool Things about this Ocean

1:_____

2: _____

3: _____

4: _____

Ocean Fact File: Pacific

Color the location of the Atlantic Ocean on the Map.

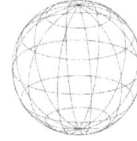

Hemisphere (circle one)

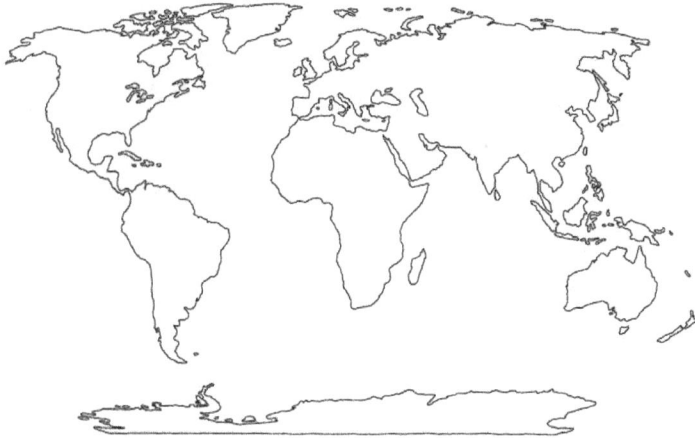

Northern

Southern

Both

FACTS

Maximum Depth:_____

Location of Deepest Point: _____

Warmest Temperature: _____

Coldest Temperature: _____

Other Cool Things about this Ocean

1:_____

2: _____

3: _____

4: _____

Ocean Fact File: Indian

Color the location of the Atlantic Ocean on the Map.

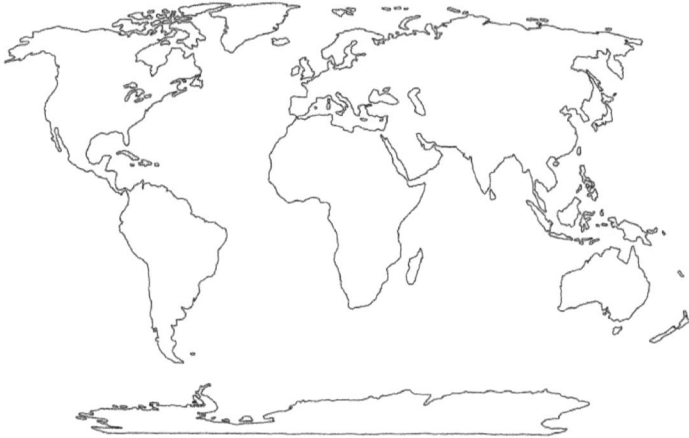

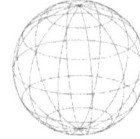

Hemisphere
(circle one)

Northern

Southern

Both

FACTS

Maximum Depth:_____

Location of Deepest Point: _____

Warmest Temperature: _____

Coldest Temperature: _____

Other Cool Things about this Ocean

1:_____

2: _____

3: _____

4: _____

Ocean Fact File: Arctic

Color the location of the Atlantic Ocean on the Map.

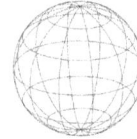

Hemisphere
(circle one)

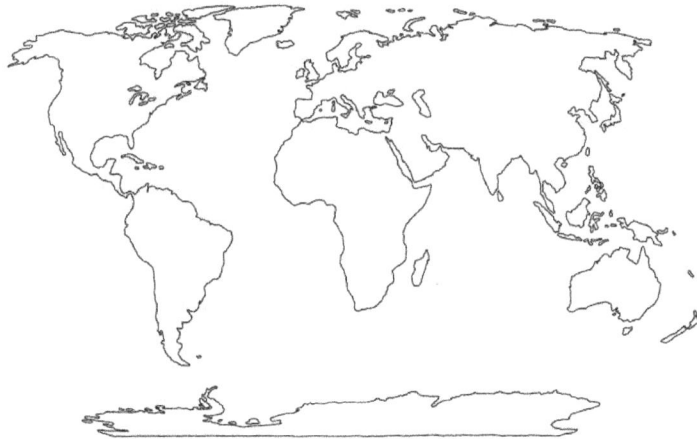

Northern

Southern

Both

FACTS

Maximum Depth:_____

Location of Deepest Point: _____

Warmest Temperature: _____

Coldest Temperature: _____

Other Cool Things about this Ocean

1:_____

2: _____

3: _____

4: _____

Ocean Fact File: Southern

Color the location of the Atlantic Ocean on the Map.

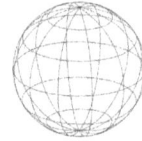

Hemisphere
(circle one)

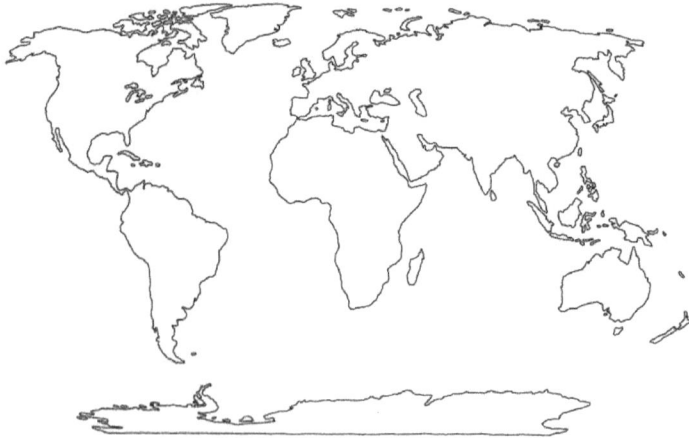

Northern

Southern

Both

FACTS

Maximum Depth:_____

Location of Deepest Point: _____

Warmest Temperature: _____

Coldest Temperature: _____

Other Cool Things about this Ocean

1:_____

2: _____

3: _____

4: _____

Antarctica

Books about Antarctica

1. (O) *Lonely Planet Antarctica (Country Guide)* by Alexis Averbuck

2. (O) *Endurance: Shackleton's Incredible Voyage* by Alfred Lansing

3. (Y) *Antarctica* by Helen Cowcher

4. (Y) *Where Is Antarctica?* by Sarah Fabini

5. (O) *Alone in Antarctica: The First Woman to Ski Solo Across the Southern Ice* by Felicity Aston

6. (Y) *The Endurance: Shackleton's Perilous Expedition in Antarctica* by Meredith Hooper

* (O) books are for older readers; (Y) books are for younger readers

Movies about Antarctica

1. **Frozen Planet** (2011)(PG-13)

2. **Penguins** (2019)(G)

3. **The Endurance: Shackleton's Legendary Antarctic Expedition** (2000)

4. **Encounters at the end of the World** (2007)

5. **Happy Feet** (2006)(PG)

6. **Antarctica: A Year on Ice** (2013)(PG)

7. **March of the Penguins** (2005)(PG)

8. **Ice and the Sky** (2015)

YouTube videos about Antarctica General

- The Land of Pure Silence | Continent 7: Antarctica

    - https://www.youtube.com/watch?v=35QEU09XHxU

- When Antarctica Was Green

    - https://www.youtube.com/watch?v=cC4WiBCoVeo

- The Secrets of Antarctica | Full Documentary | TRACKS

    - https://www.youtube.com/watch?v=sbYX4Lur4Yc

- Why Planes Don't Fly Over Antarctica

    - https://www.youtube.com/watch?v=dpzX5MJQybw

- SOUTH POLE | NIGHT IN ANTARCTICA

    - https://www.youtube.com/watch?v=t57DPnH06V0

- The Arctic vs. the Antarctic - Camille Seaman

    - https://www.youtube.com/watch?v=Z5VRoGTF60s

- The Logistics of Living in Antarctica

    - https://www.youtube.com/watch?v=-s3j-ptJD10

- McMurdo Station, Antarctica a Typical Day

    - https://www.youtube.com/watch?v=gVwAOhWYHvw

- Who Actually Owns Antarctica?

    - https://www.youtube.com/watch?v=Xp_vWnn6H3k

Continent Fact File: Antarctica

Population:_____

Area: _____

Highest Point: _____

Longest River: _____

Tallest Waterfall: _____

Number of Countries: _____

Largest Country: _____

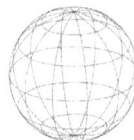

Hemisphere
(circle one)

Northern

Southern

Both

Major
Biomes

1:_____

2: _____

3: _____

 Other Cool Things about this Continent

1:_____

2: _____

3: _____

4: _____

Map it Out: Antarctica

Color and Label the following on the map of Antarctica:

- ❑ South Pole
- ❑ Atlantic Ocean
- ❑ Southern Ocean
- ❑ Pacific Ocean
- ❑ Indian Ocean

- ❑ Weddel Sea
- ❑ Ross Sea
- ❑ Ronne Ice Shelf
- ❑ Ross Shelf

Bases of Antarctica

Antarctica is home to research facilities belonging to many different countries. Research 6 different countries and mark the location of a base used by that country on the map above. Then add the county to the legend below.

Legend:

Animals of Antarctica

Fill out the following boxes with animals that are native to **Antarctica**

Animal Common Name
_____

Scientific Name
_____

List 3 facts about this animal

1. _____
   _____

2. _____
   _____

3. _____
   _____

Animal Common Name
_____

Scientific Name
_____

List 3 facts about this animal

1. _____
   _____

2. _____
   _____

3. _____
   _____

Animal Common Name
_____

Scientific Name
_____

List 3 facts about this animal

1. _____
   _____

2. _____
   _____

3. _____
   _____

Animal Common Name
_____

Scientific Name
_____

List 3 facts about this animal

1. _____
   _____

2. _____
   _____

3. _____
   _____

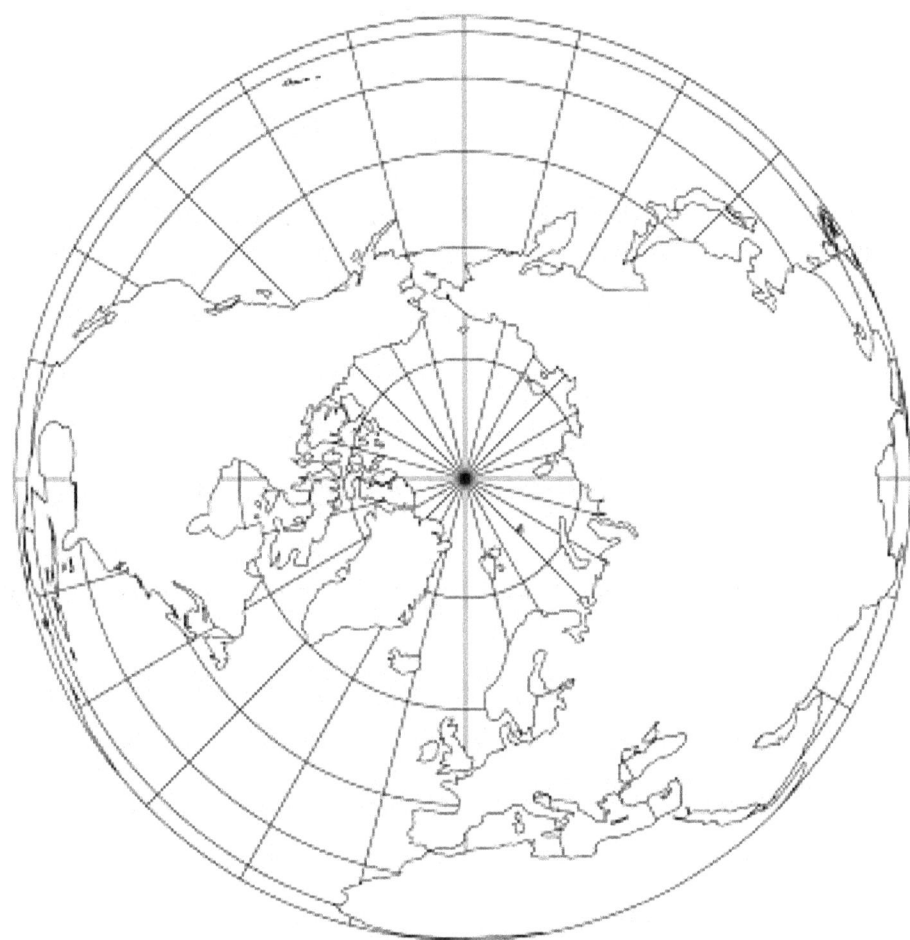

The Artic Circle

Books about the Arctic

1. (O) *Sea, Ice and Rock: Sailing and Climbing Above the Arctic Circle* by Chris Bonington

2. (O) *Arctic Dreams* by Barry Lopez

3. (O) *Ice Bear: The Cultural History of an Arctic Icon* by Michael Engelhard

4. (Y) *Here Is the Arctic Winter (Web of Life)* by Madeline Dunphy

5. (Y*) North: The Amazing Story of Arctic Migration* by Nick Dowson

6. (Y) *Arctic Tundra* by Donald Silver

* (O) books are for older readers; (Y) books are for younger readers

Movies about the Arctic

1. **Arctic** (2018)(PG-13)

2. **Arctic Dogs** (2019)(PG)

3. **To the Arctic 3D** (2012)(G)

4. **Norm of the North** (2016)(PG)

5. **Arctic Tale** (2007)(G)

6. **Long Way North** (2015)(PG)

YouTube videos about the Artic

- Who Owns The Arctic Ocean?

  - https://www.youtube.com/watch?v=pk9Z7xrRCRY

- Could we urbanize the ARCTIC? (Geography Now!)

  - https://www.youtube.com/watch?v=3Z_7NR7a0LE

- Life in the Arctic Circle - Northern Norway

  - https://www.youtube.com/watch?v=kl28cbwSq5U

- The Arctic Circle Is Losing A Country (All Arctic Countries)

  - https://www.youtube.com/watch?v=8V4iai5YkTo

- ARCTIC CIRCLE || Mapping, Issues, Analysis, Arctic Council, Climate Change | World Geography Mapping

  - https://www.youtube.com/watch?v=xViG6ooUrAs

Map it Out: The Artic Circle

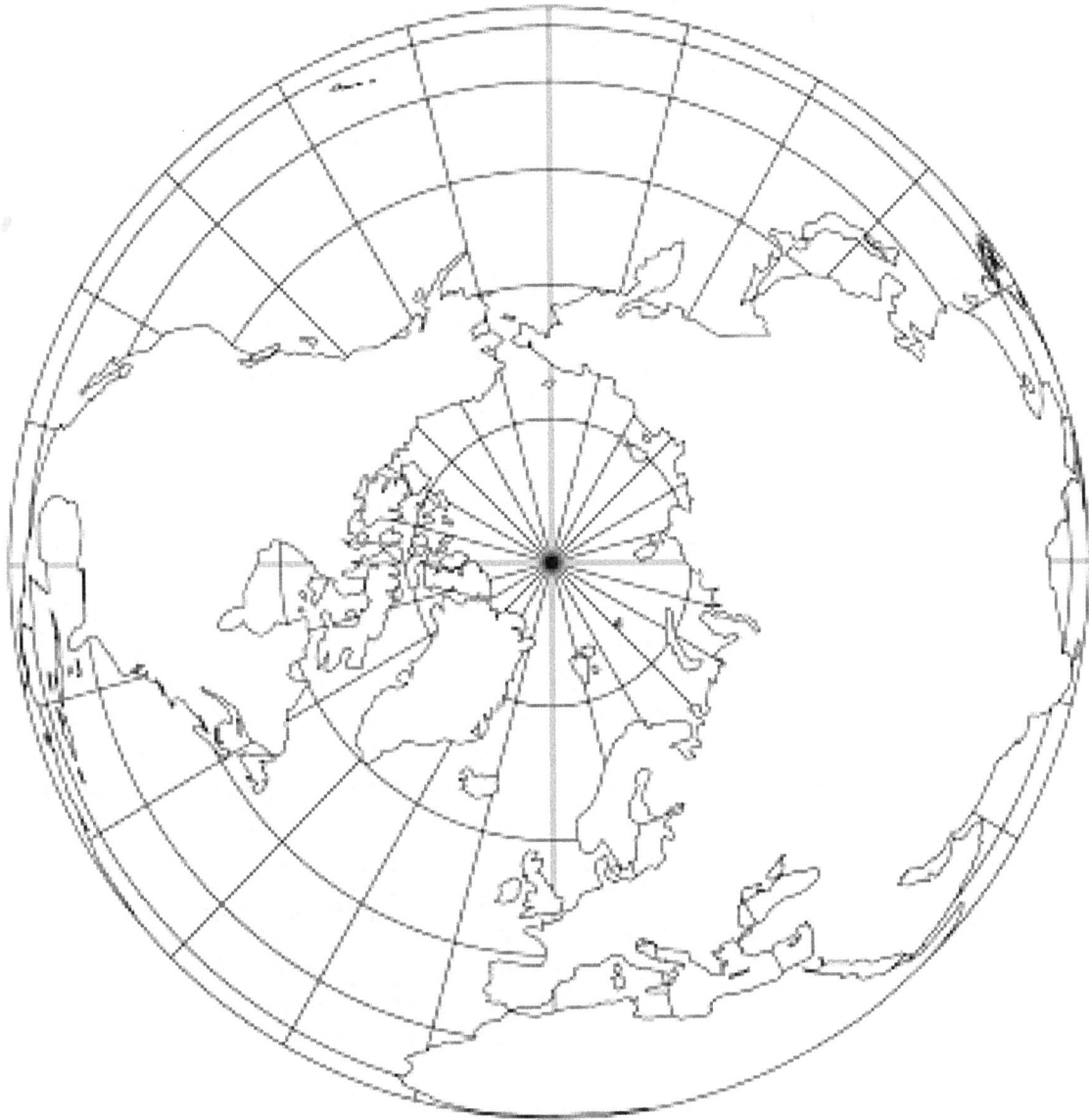

Color and Label the following on the map of the Arctic Circle:

- ❑ Arctic ocean
- ❑ Atlantic Ocean
- ❑ Pacific Ocean
- ❑ Greenland
- ❑ Russia

- ❑ Canada
- ❑ United States
- ❑ Europe

Animals of The Arctic Circle

Fill out the following boxes with animals that are native to **the Arctic Circle**

Animal Common Name

_____

Scientific Name

_____

List 3 facts about this animal

1. _____

   _____

2. _____

   _____

3. _____

   _____

Animal Common Name

_____

Scientific Name

_____

List 3 facts about this animal

1. _____

   _____

2. _____

   _____

3. _____

   _____

Animal Common Name

_____

Scientific Name

_____

List 3 facts about this animal

1. _____

   _____

2. _____

   _____

3. _____

   _____

Animal Common Name

_____

Scientific Name

_____

List 3 facts about this animal

1. _____

   _____

2. _____

   _____

3. _____

   _____

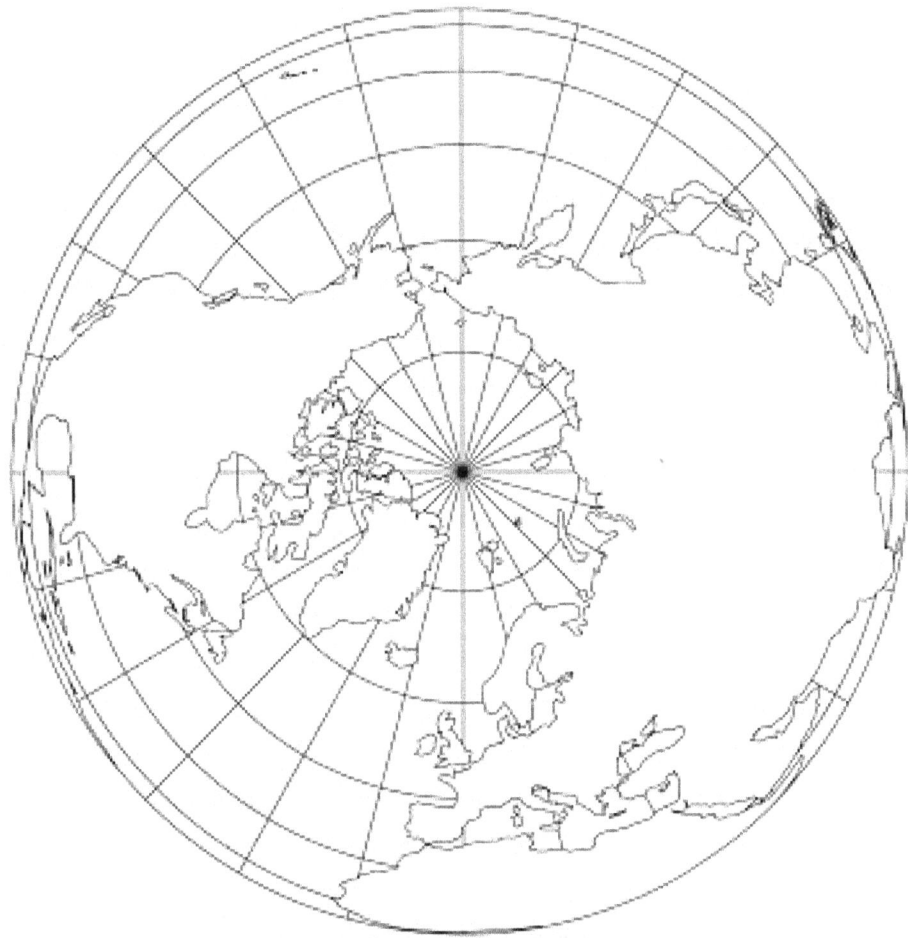

Pole Vs Pole

Books about The Earth's Poles

1. (O) ***Polar Dream: The First Solo Expedition by a Woman and Her Dog to the Magnetic North Pole*** by Helen Thayer

2. (O) ***North Pole, South Pole: The Epic Quest to Solve the Great Mystery of Earth's Magnetism*** by Gillian Turner

3. (Y) ***All About the North and South Poles (Habitats)*** by Christina Mia Gardeski

4. (Y) ***Ice Is Nice!: All About the North and South Poles (Cat in the Hat's Learning Library)*** by Bonnie Worth

Games about the Earth's Poles

1. Penguins on Ice (Smart Games)
2. Don't Break the Ice
3. Pressman Thin Ice Game - Don't Let Your Marble Be The One That Breaks The Ice,
4. PlayMonster Yeti in My Spaghetti

* (O) books are for older readers; (Y) books are for younger readers

YouTube Videos about The Magnetic Earth

- Planetary Poles and Magnetic Fields - Sixty Symbols

  - https://www.youtube.com/watch?v=EoqBp2nW5rg

- Earth and Compasses | Magnetism | Physics | FuseSchool

  - https://www.youtube.com/watch?v=OsQNHFlF8w4

- Magnetic Field

  - https://www.youtube.com/watch?v=vgWiBYuPpjw

- Magnetism | The Dr. Binocs Show | Educational Videos For Kids

  - https://www.youtube.com/watch?v=yXCeuSiTOug

- Working of Compass | Earth as Magnet | Magnetic & Geographic Poles

  - https://www.youtube.com/watch?v=PcuDZThGZ-k

- What if Earth's Magnetic Poles Flipped?

  - https://www.youtube.com/watch?v=6MvKHIKCYN4

How Earth is Like a Magnet

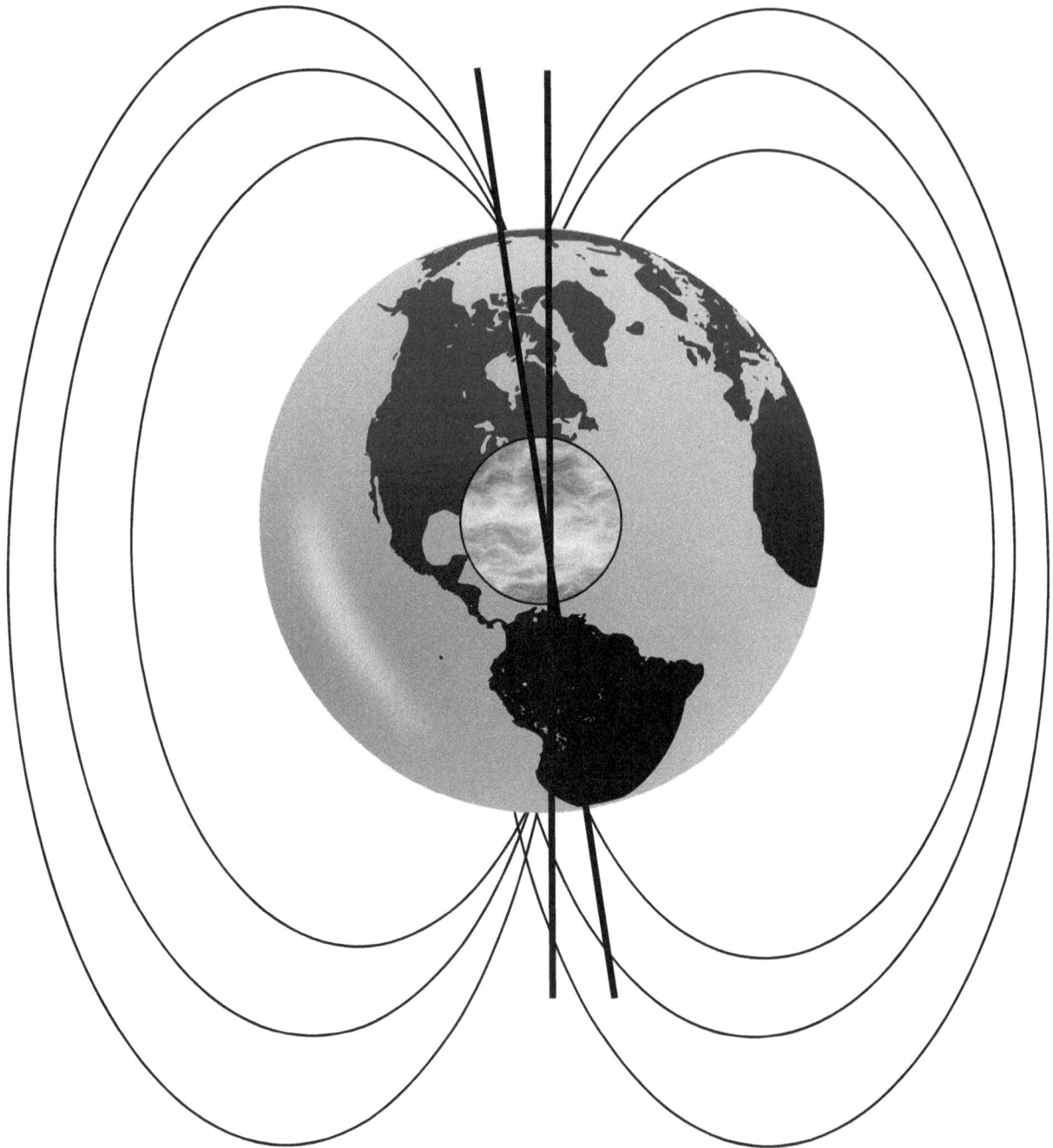

Directions: Label the following on the diagram above: **geographic poles magnetic poles, magnetic field, core**

Pole vs Pole

Complete the Venn Diagram comparing the Arctic Circle to Antarctica.

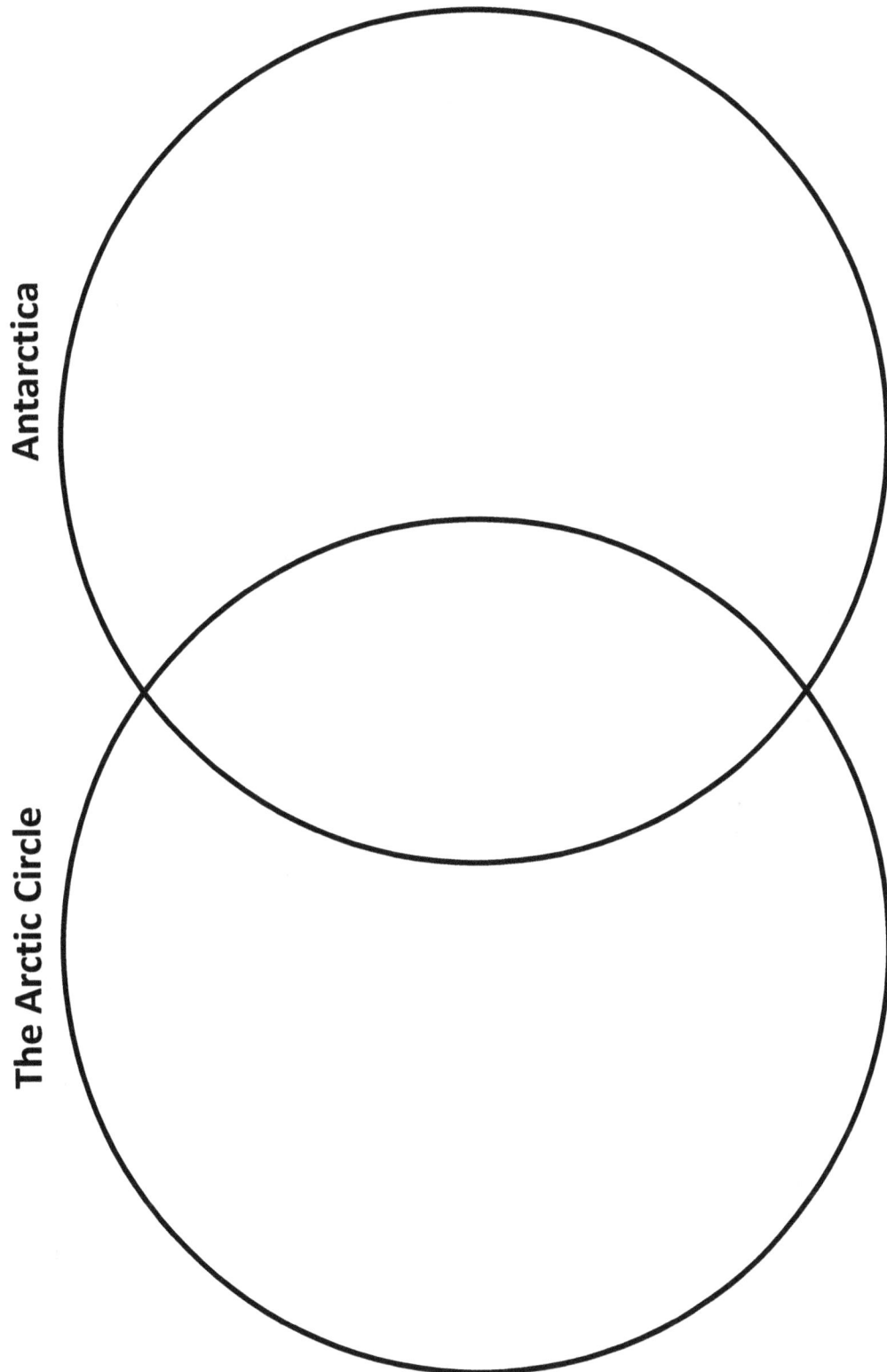

Antarctica

The Arctic Circle

Animals of the Poles

Complete the Venn Diagram listing animals found in the Arctic Circle, Antarctica or both.

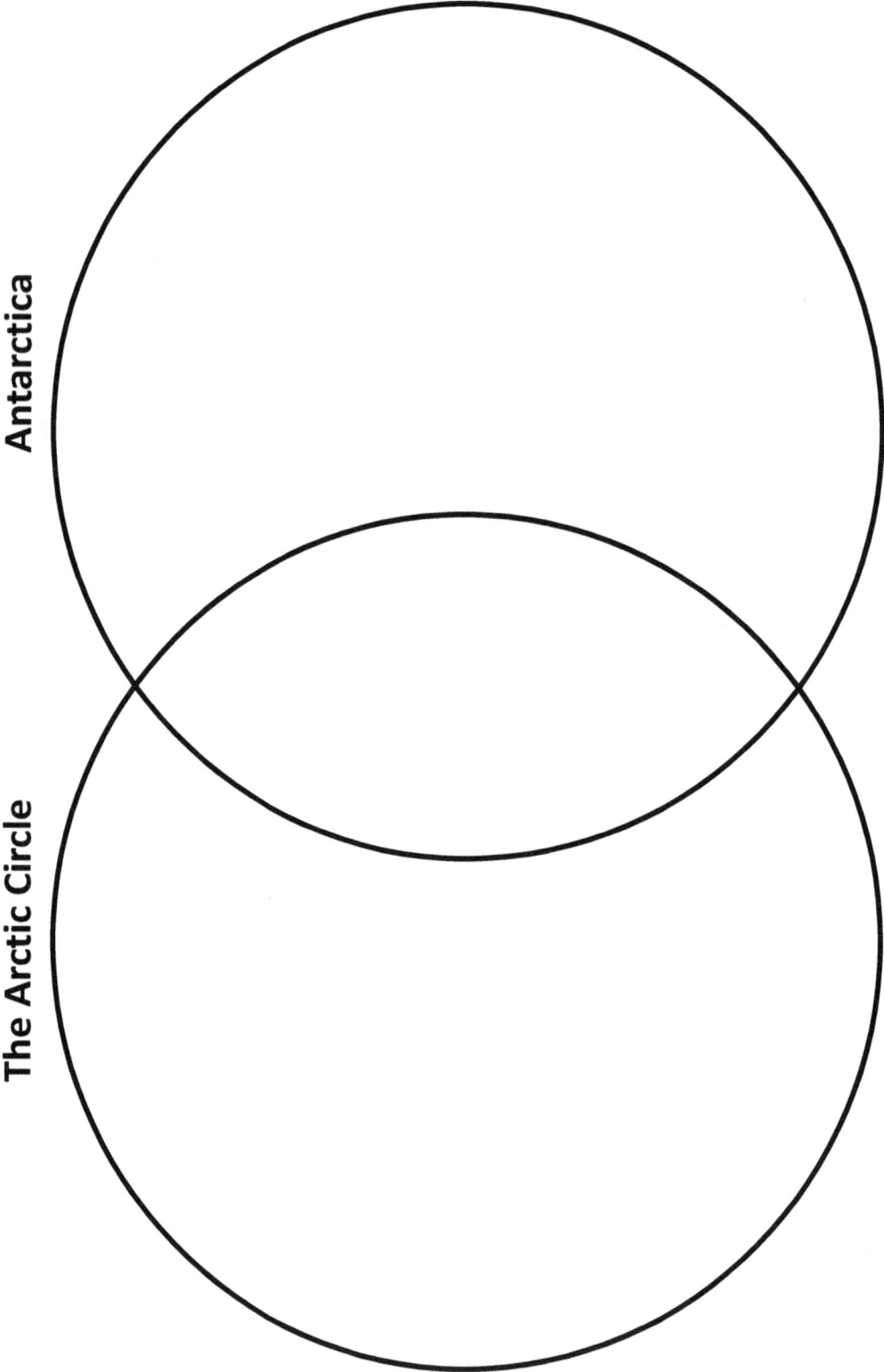

Antarctica

The Arctic Circle

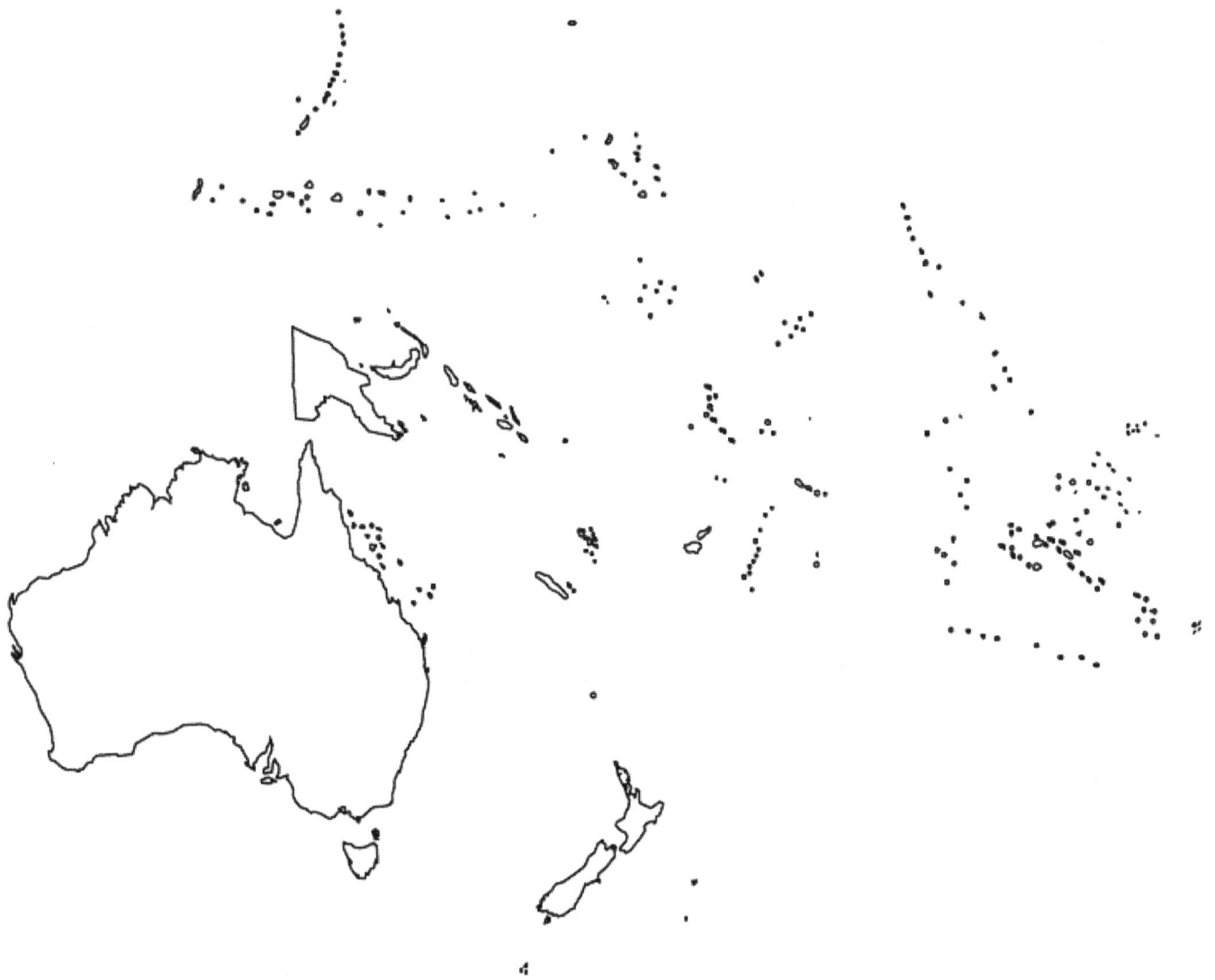

Australia and Oceana

Books about Australia and Oceana

1. (Y) ***DK Eyewitness Australia (Travel Guide)*** by DK Eyewitness

2. (Y) ***An Aussie Year: Twelve Months in the Life of Australian Kids***

   by Tania McCartney and Tina Snerling

3. (O) ***The Dogs that Made Australia: The Story of the Dogs that Brought about Australia's Transformation from Starving Colony to Pastoral Powerhouse*** by Guy Hull

4. (O) ***Australia: History of Australia: Discover the major events that shaped the history of Australia*** by James Walker

Games about Australia and Oceana

1. Wombat Rescue

2. AuZtralia

3. Australia's Deadly Animals Bingo

4. KAADOO - The Classic Big Game to Explore Australian Wilderness

Movies about Australia and Oceana

1. Rabbit Proof Fence (2002)(PG)

2. Crocodile Dundee (1986) (PG-13)

3. 10 Canoes (2006)(Not Rated)

4. Rogue Nation (2008)(Not Rated)

5. Storm Boy (1976) (Not Rated)

6. Babe (1995)(G)

7. The Rescuers Down Under (1990)(G)

8. Moana(2016)(G)

9. *Finding Nemo(2003)*(G)

10. Cast Away(2000)(PG-13)

YouTube Playlist about the Continent of Australia and Oceana

Australia

- Australia: Country or Continent?
  - https://www.youtube.com/watch?v=Hhe9zTmKVz8
- Oceania and Antarctica Geography Made Easy
  - https://www.youtube.com/watch?v=yAhS8ID_QrI

Oceana

- OCEANIA EXPLAINED (Geography Now!)
  - https://www.youtube.com/watch?v=Cj1mJGTmLRs
- Map of Oceania, Oceania Continent [Location of Countries and Islands]
  - https://www.youtube.com/watch?v=fKp5aqQ5mSQ

Continent Fact File: Australia and Oceana

Population:_____

Area: _____

Highest Point: _____

Longest River: _____

Tallest Waterfall: _____

Number of countries:

_____

Largest Country: _____

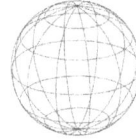

Hemisphere
(circle one)

Northern

Southern

Both

Major
Biomes

1:_____

2: _____

3: _____

 Other Cool Things about this Continent

1:_____

2: _____

3: _____

4: _____

Map it Out: Australia and Oceana

Color and Label the following on the map of Australia and Oceana:

- ❑ Indian Ocean,
- ❑ Pacific Ocean,
- ❑ Philippine Sea,
- ❑ Tasman Sea,
- ❑ Coral Sea

- ❑ Uluru
- ❑ Great Barrier Reef
- ❑ Mount Kosciuszko
- ❑ Ring of Fire

World Wonders in Australia and Oceana

7 Wonders of the World

Wonders of the natural world

- **Great Barrier Reef (Australia)**
  - Great Barrier Reef | Exploring Oceans
    - https://www.youtube.com/watch?v=wbNeIn3vVKM
  - Australia's Great Barrier Reef [National Geographic Documentary 2020 HD]
    - https://www.youtube.com/watch?v=ZNAH1Fu9Ung
  - How Scientists Are Restoring The Great Barrier Reef | Travel + Leisure
    - https://www.youtube.com/watch?v=8hknaJQRh8s
  - The Great Barrier Reef: what's the value of Australia's natural wonder?
    - https://www.youtube.com/watch?v=HgIw-HhwAFA

Wonders of the World: Great Barrier Reef

Draw a Picture of the wonder.

Mark the Location on the Map of Australia and Oceana

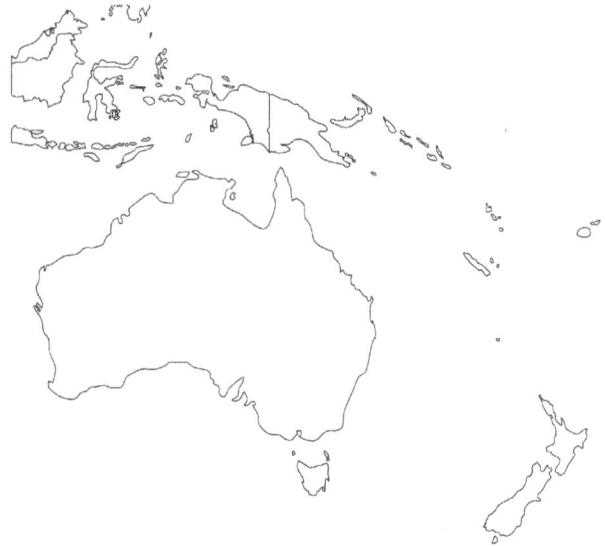

This is a (circle one):	Original Wonder of the World	New Wonder of the World	Wonder of the Natural World

Write a description of the wonder:

Why is it considered a wonder of the world?

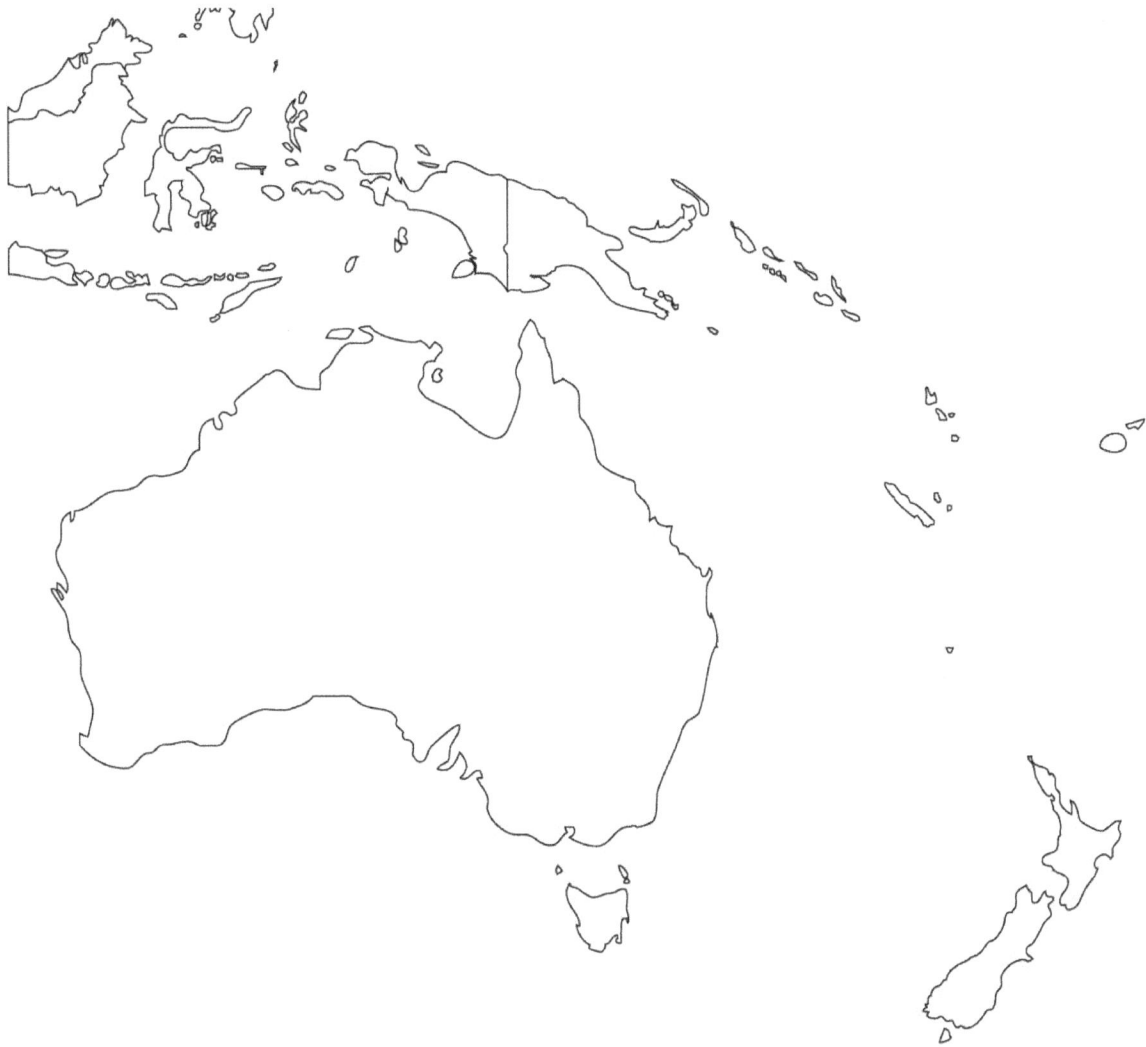

Countries of Australia and Oceana

Countries of Australia and Oceana

1. Australia
2. Fiji
3. Kiribati
4. Marshal Islands
5. Micronesia
6. Nauru
7. New Zealand
8. Palau
9. Papua New Guinea
10. Samoa
11. Solomon Islands
12. Tonga
13. Tuvalu
14. Vanuatu

Countries of Australia and Oceana

Australia

- Geography Now! Australia
  - https://www.youtube.com/watch?v=ynHIlx5RgtI
- AUSTRALIA- States and territories explained (Geography Now!)
  - https://www.youtube.com/watch?v=yrYnTgB3bn8

Fiji

- Geography Now! FIJI
  - https://www.youtube.com/watch?v=AFf22L5ZZN4
- Flag Friday FIJI! (Geography Now)
  - https://www.youtube.com/watch?v=pRoKQOthaqw
- A-Z Documentaries - Best Documentary about Fiji
  - https://www.youtube.com/watch?v=7yj_Nmtl9e4

Kiribati

- Geography Now! Kiribati
  - https://www.youtube.com/watch?v=ZtoZlLj8t1c
- Flag Fan Friday KIRIBATI! (Geography Now!)
  - https://www.youtube.com/watch?v=glyateCsn_I
- Life in Kiribati..Remote Survival
  - https://www.youtube.com/watch?v=41MzOyZvMJw

Marshal Islands

- Geography Now! MARSHALL ISLANDS
  - https://www.youtube.com/watch?v=wRzXi8DDrX8
- Flag / Fan Friday MARSHALL ISLANDS! (Geography Now!)
  - https://www.youtube.com/watch?v=0hhTBkISip0
- The Marshall Islands, a nation that fears it's on the brink of extinction
  - https://www.youtube.com/watch?v=qZUDdAs2ME0

Countries of Australia and Oceana

Micronesia

- Geography Now! MICRONESIA (Federated states)
  - https://www.youtube.com/watch?v=_gSBvcYOuu4
- Flag/ Fan Friday MICRONESIA (Geography Now!)
  - https://www.youtube.com/watch?v=w8SLYpexB7U
- The Truth about Living in Micronesia (Kosrae, Pohnpei, Yap, Chuuk, etc)
  - https://www.youtube.com/watch?v=s40JOTS4Qlg

Nauru

- Geography Now! NAURU
  - https://www.youtube.com/watch?v=B5fIHIEkgrU
- Flag/ Fan Friday NAURU (Geography Now)
  - https://www.youtube.com/watch?v=QD0pkHAjlEs
- INSIDE NAURU - The World's Least Visited Vountry
  - https://www.youtube.com/watch?v=7WKEZPF489U

New Zealand

- Geography Now! NEW ZEALAND (AOTEAROA)
  - https://www.youtube.com/watch?v=FtZaaKFi7RM
- Flag / Fan Friday NEW ZEALAND (Geography Now!)
  - https://www.youtube.com/watch?v=Oz7boqoIQOU
- Entire History of New Zealand II History Quickly
  - https://www.youtube.com/watch?v=IMWk2CtUVKs

Countries of Australia and Oceana

Palau

- Geography Now! PALAU
  - https://www.youtube.com/watch?v=MOM09fA8miU&t=441s
- Flag/ Fan Friday PALAU! (Geography Now!)
  - https://www.youtube.com/watch?v=AnieKbQo5Kg
- Palau is an Island Paradise Standing up to the World
  - https://www.youtube.com/watch?v=qrA56-VypuM

Papua New Guinea

- Geography Now! PAPUA NEW GUINEA
  - https://www.youtube.com/watch?v=bushHvw__Mo
- Flag/ Fan Friday PAPUA NEW GUINEA (Geography Now!)
  - https://www.youtube.com/watch?v=isG2gEQM88Q
- Deep in: Papua New Guinea | Short Documentary (2019)
  - https://www.youtube.com/watch?v=BBnCujiom5k

Samoa

- Geography Now! SAMOA
  - https://www.youtube.com/watch?v=vEt3jg2XTO4
- Flag/ Fan Friday SAMOA (Geography Now!)
  - https://www.youtube.com/watch?v=KGRrgXAPw1Q
- The Difference Between Samoa, American Samoa and the Samoan Islands Explained
  - https://www.youtube.com/watch?v=4Xv2a79YH_Y
- Samoana Documentary
  - https://www.youtube.com/watch?v=yCpUhY-eH4U

Countries of Australia and Oceana

Solomon Islands

- National Geographic - The Solomon Islands
    - https://www.youtube.com/watch?v=Oa0FL1pBg7o
- Surprising Facts about the Scattered Solomon Islands
    - https://www.youtube.com/watch?v=YEjZzKZfJO8
- Villages and Culture in the Solomon Islands
    - https://www.youtube.com/watch?v=QyHBx_Us76k

Tonga

- Geography of Tonga Explained
    - https://www.youtube.com/watch?v=qPP24-E69KA
- Zooming in on TONGA | Geography of Tonga with Google Earth
    - https://www.youtube.com/watch?v=KvT9nhl5Uzs
- Discover these facts about Tonga
    - https://www.youtube.com/watch?v=dCed_owif10

Tuvalu

- Zooming in on TUVALU | Geography of Tuvalu with Google Earth
    - https://www.youtube.com/watch?v=oWNgNpncL7I
- Things Worth Knowing about Tuvalu
    - https://www.youtube.com/watch?v=TWLlqOz76Ms
- Tuvalu will be 'Uninhabitable Before it Goes under Water'
    - https://www.youtube.com/watch?v=WnohiusCDXY

Countries of Australia and Oceana

Vanuatu

- Zooming in on Vanuatu | Geography of Vanuatu with Google Earth
  - https://www.youtube.com/watch?v=lSh82DX9uG8

- The History of Vanuatu
  - https://www.youtube.com/watch?v=-kBrCueZg1k

- Glamorous Vanuatu: 'The Happiest Place on Earth'
  - https://www.youtube.com/watch?v=_70Ff_jCi3g

Australia

Color the country's flag in the box above.

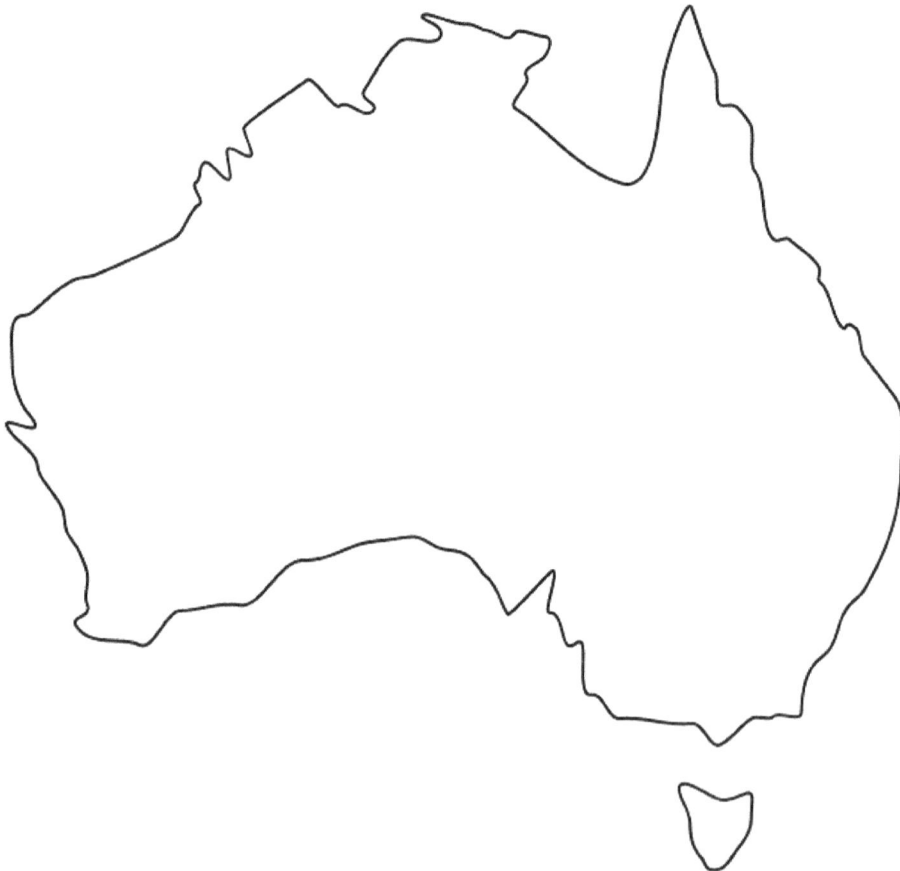

Label the capital city and any major physical features such as mountains, rivers, oceans or seas **in or around** this country.

Country Name: Australia

FACTS

Population:_____

Area: _____

Type of Government: _____

Capital City: _____

Religion(s): _____

Language(s): _____

Currency: _____

Climate: _____

Time Zone: _____

Major Exports

1:_____

2:_____

3:_____

Mountains, Rivers and Lakes

1:_____

2:_____

3:_____

Other Cool Things about this Country

1:_____

2:_____

3:_____

4:_____

Fiji

Color the country's flag in the box above.

Label the capital city and any major physical features such as mountains, rivers, oceans or seas **in or around** this country.

Country Name: Fiji

FACTS

Population:_____

Area: _____

Type of Government: _____

Capital City: _____

Religion(s): _____

Language(s): _____

Currency: _____

Climate: _____

Time Zone: _____

Major Exports

1:_____

2: _____

3: _____

Mountains, Rivers and Lakes

1:_____

2: _____

3: _____

Other Cool Things about this Country

1:_____

2: _____

3: _____

4: _____

Kiribati

Color the country's flag in the box above.

Label the capital city and any major physical features such as mountains, rivers, oceans or seas **in or around** this country.

Country Name: Kiribati

FACTS

Population:_____

Area: _____

Type of Government: _____

Capital City: _____

Religion(s): _____

Language(s): _____

Currency: _____

Climate: _____

Time Zone: _____

Major Exports

1:_____

2: _____

3: _____

Mountains, Rivers and Lakes

1:_____

2: _____

3: _____

Other Cool Things about this Country

1:_____

2: _____

3: _____

4: _____

Marshal Islands

Color the country's flag in the box above.

Label the capital city and any major physical features such as mountains, rivers, oceans or seas **in or around** this country.

Country Name: Marshal Islands

FACTS

Population:_____

Area: _____

Type of Government: _____

Capital City: _____

Religion(s): _____

Language(s): _____

Currency: _____

Climate: _____

Time Zone: _____

Major Exports

1:_____

2: _____

3: _____

Mountains, Rivers and Lakes

1:_____

2: _____

3: _____

Other Cool Things about this Country

1:_____

2: _____

3: _____

4: _____

Micronesia

Color the country's flag in the box above.

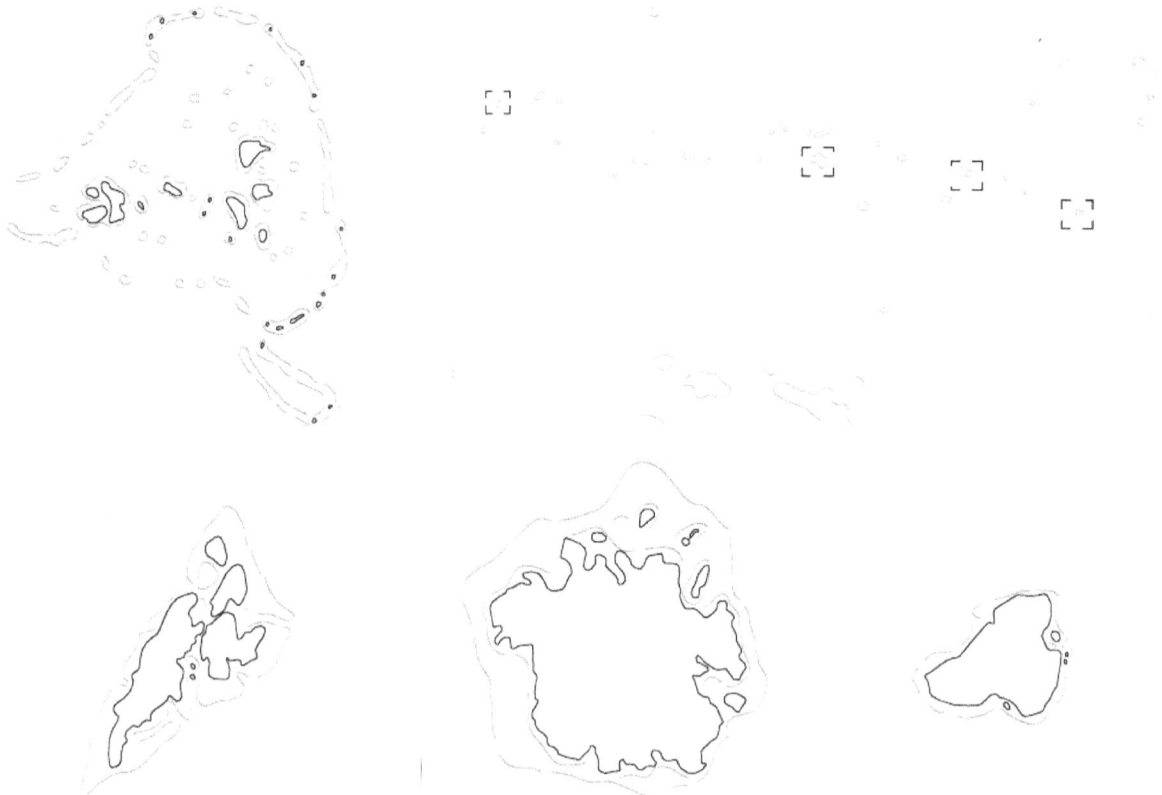

Label the capital city and any major physical features such as mountains, rivers, oceans or seas **in or around** this country.

Country Name: Micronesia

FACTS

Population:_____

Area: _____

Type of Government: _____

Capital City: _____

Religion(s): _____

Language(s): _____

Currency: _____

Climate: _____

Time Zone: _____

Major Exports

1:_____

2: _____

3: _____

Mountains, Rivers and Lakes

1:_____

2: _____

3: _____

Other Cool Things about this Country

1:_____

2: _____

3: _____

4: _____

Nauru

Color the country's flag in the box above.

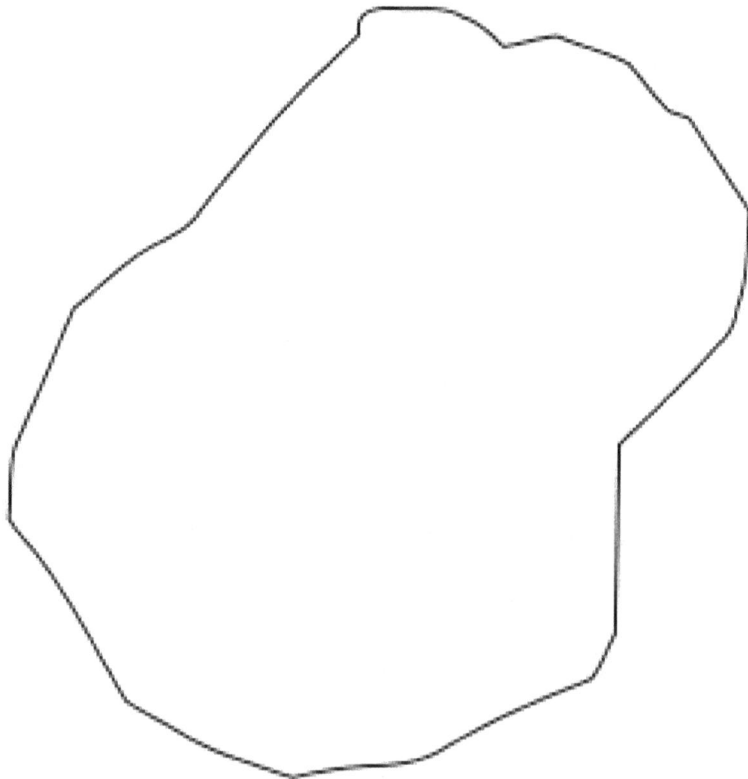

Label the capital city and any major physical features such as mountains, rivers, oceans or seas **in or around** this country.

Country Name: Nauru

FACTS

Population:_____

Area: _____

Type of Government: _____

Capital City: _____

Religion(s): _____

Language(s): _____

Currency: _____

Climate: _____

Time Zone: _____

Major Exports

1:_____

2: _____

3: _____

Mountains, Rivers and Lakes

1:_____

2: _____

3: _____

Other Cool Things about this Country

1:_____

2: _____

3: _____

4: _____

New Zealand

Color the country's flag in the box above.

Label the capital city and any major physical features such as mountains, rivers, oceans or seas **in or around** this country.

Country Name: New Zealand

FACTS

Population:_____

Area: _____

Type of Government: _____

Capital City: _____

Religion(s): _____

Language(s): _____

Currency: _____

Climate: _____

Time Zone: _____

Major Exports

1:_____

2:_____

3:_____

Mountains, Rivers and Lakes

1:_____

2:_____

3:_____

Other Cool Things about this Country

1:_____

2:_____

3:_____

4:_____

Palau

Color the country's flag in the box above.

Label the capital city and any major physical features such as mountains, rivers, oceans or seas **in or around** this country.

Country Name: Palau

FACTS

Population:_____

Area: _____

Type of Government: _____

Capital City: _____

Religion(s): _____

Language(s): _____

Currency: _____

Climate: _____

Time Zone: _____

Major Exports

1:_____

2: _____

3: _____

Mountains, Rivers and Lakes

1:_____

2: _____

3: _____

Other Cool Things about this Country

1:_____

2: _____

3: _____

4: _____

Papua New Guinea

Color the country's flag in the box above.

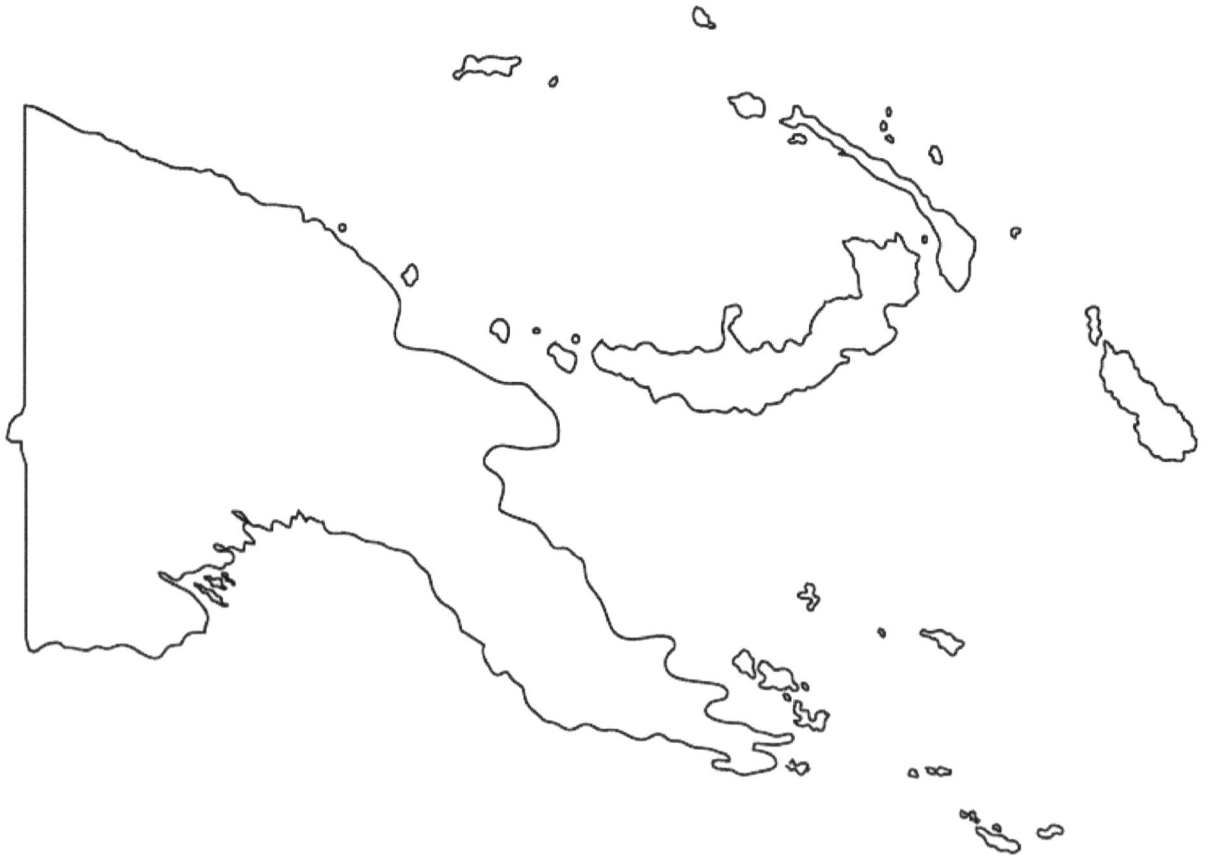

Label the capital city and any major physical features such as mountains, rivers, oceans or seas **in or around** this country.

Country Name: Papua New Guinea

FACTS

Population:_____

Area: _____

Type of Government: _____

Capital City: _____

Religion(s): _____

Language(s): _____

Currency: _____

Climate: _____

Time Zone: _____

Major Exports

1:_____

2: _____

3: _____

Mountains, Rivers and Lakes

1:_____

2: _____

3: _____

Other Cool Things about this Country

1:_____

2: _____

3: _____

4: _____

Samoa

Color the country's flag in the box above.

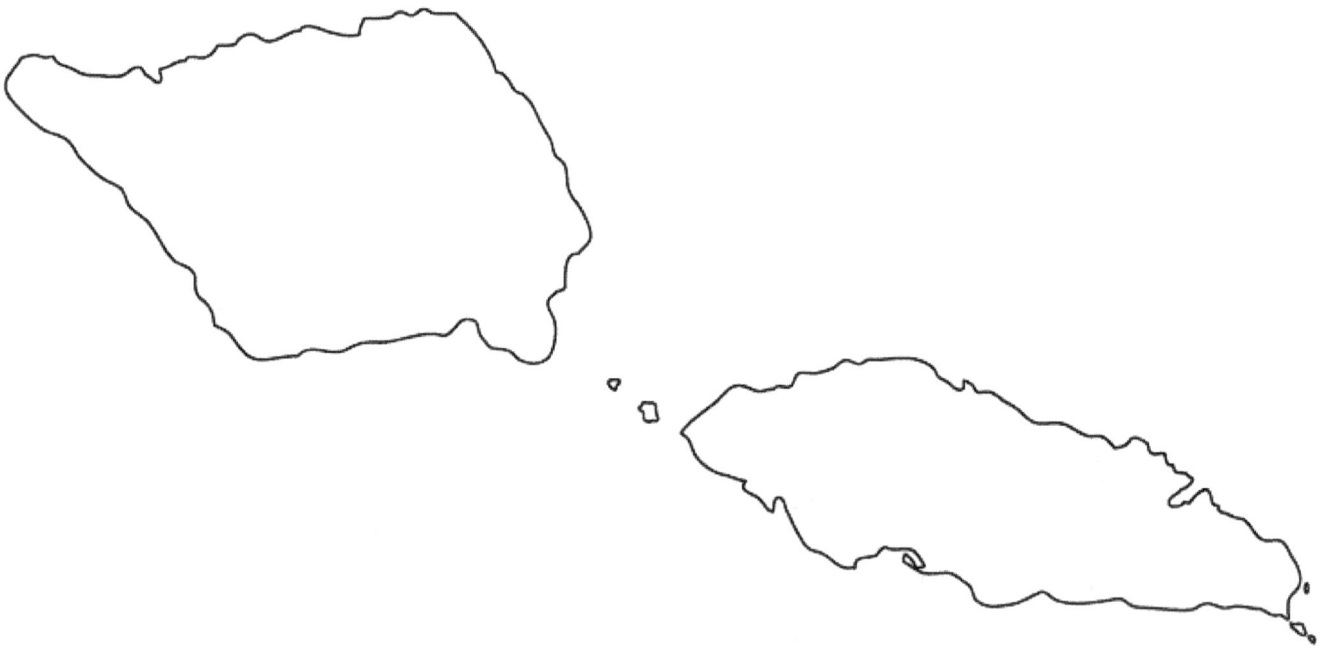

Label the capital city and any major physical features such as mountains, rivers, oceans or seas **in or around** this country.

Country Name: Samoa

FACTS

Population:_____

Area: _____

Type of Government: _____

Capital City: _____

Religion(s): _____

Language(s): _____

Currency: _____

Climate: _____

Time Zone: _____

Major Exports

1:_____

2: _____

3: _____

Mountains, Rivers and Lakes

1:_____

2: _____

3: _____

Other Cool Things about this Country

1:_____

2: _____

3: _____

4: _____

Solomon Islands

Color the country's flag in the box above.

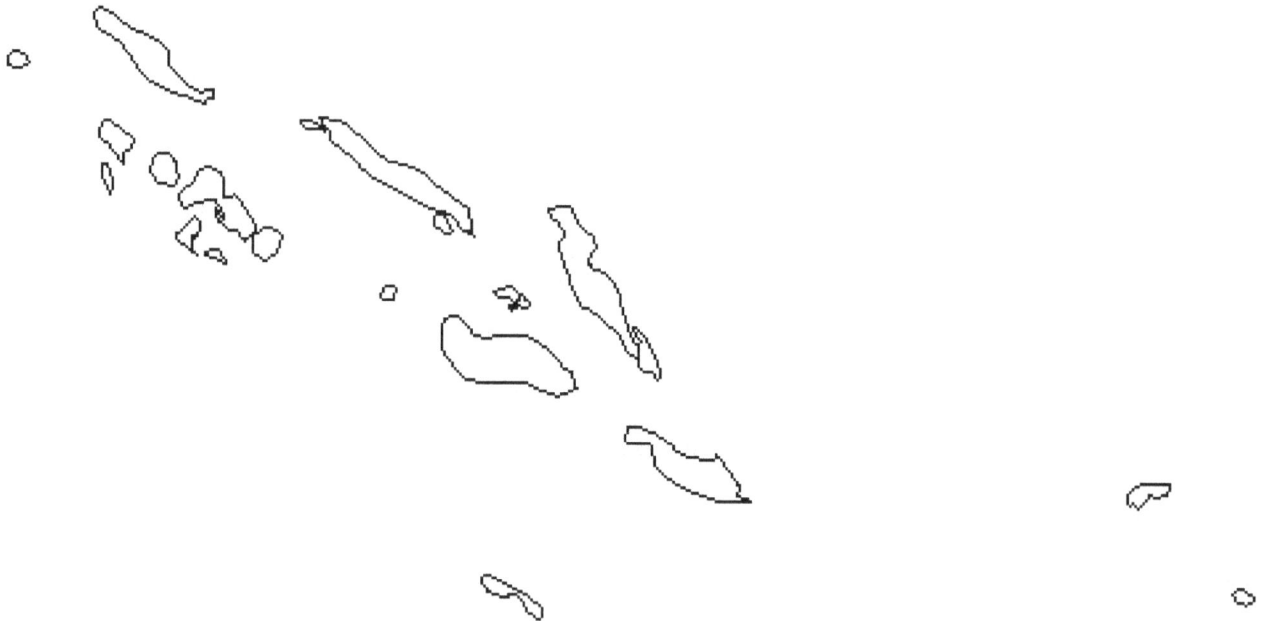

Label the capital city and any major physical features such as mountains, rivers, oceans or seas **in or around** this country.

Country Name: Solomon Islands

FACTS

Population:_____

Area: _____

Type of Government: _____

Capital City: _____

Religion(s): _____

Language(s): _____

Currency: _____

Climate: _____

Time Zone: _____

Major Exports

1:_____

2: _____

3: _____

Mountains, Rivers and Lakes

1:_____

2: _____

3: _____

Other Cool Things about this Country

1:_____

2: _____

3: _____

4: _____

Tonga

Color the country's flag in the box above.

Label the capital city and any major physical features such as mountains, rivers, oceans or seas **in or around** this country.

Country Name: Tonga

FACTS

Population:_____

Area: _____

Type of Government: _____

Capital City: _____

Religion(s): _____

Language(s): _____

Currency: _____

Climate: _____

Time Zone: _____

Major Exports

1:_____

2: _____

3: _____

Mountains, Rivers and Lakes

1:_____

2: _____

3: _____

Other Cool Things about this Country

1:_____

2: _____

3: _____

4: _____

Tuvalu

Color the country's flag in the box above.

Label the capital city and any major physical features such as mountains, rivers, oceans or seas **in or around** this country.

Country Name: Tuvalu

FACTS

Population:_____

Area: _____

Type of Government: _____

Capital City: _____

Religion(s): _____

Language(s): _____

Currency: _____

Climate: _____

Time Zone: _____

Major Exports

1:_____

2:_____

3:_____

Mountains, Rivers and Lakes

1:_____

2:_____

3:_____

Other Cool Things about this Country

1:_____

2:_____

3:_____

4:_____

Vanatu

Color the country's flag in the box above.

Label the capital city and any major physical features such as mountains, rivers, oceans or seas **in or around** this country.

Country Name: Vanatu

FACTS

Population:_____

Area: _____

Type of Government: _____

Capital City: _____

Religion(s): _____

Language(s): _____

Currency: _____

Climate: _____

Time Zone: _____

Major Exports

1:_____

2:_____

3:_____

Mountains, Rivers and Lakes

1:_____

2:_____

3:_____

Other Cool Things about this Country

1:_____

2:_____

3:_____

4:_____

About Exploring Expression

My name is Brandy Champeau

I am an author, speaker and curriculum developer. Through my company, Exploring Expression, I help parents, caregivers and educators of K12 students become the very best expression of themselves so that they can make learning fun, easy and natural not just for their children, but for themselves as well.

At Exploring Expression, we focus on 4 specific offerings:

1. We build quality learning resources for K12 students
2. We create resources for parents and educators to help them become the best expressions of themselves and equip them to better facilitate learning opportunities for their children
3. We utilize public speaking platforms to spread the message of becoming the best expression of yourself through the cultivation of a learning lifestyle
4. We help people with a message find their voice, publish their books and create curriculum or training to share with the world

As you can see, our passion is learning - learning about yourself and learning about the world. We focus on self-improvement and education. Because in the end it all comes down to learning. Learning doesn't have to be hard and it doesn't have to be boring. At Exploring Expression we want to help you put the engagement and excitement back into education and to put the education back into life.

CONNECT WITH US

We would love to hear from you!

🌐 https://ExploringExpression.com

@ ExploringExpression@gmail.com

f https://www.facebook.com/ExploringExpression

📷 https://www.Instagram.com/ExploringExpression

🐦 https://www.twitter.com/ExExAdmin

📌 http://www.Pinterest.com/ExploringExpression

▶️ https://bit.ly/2KZrSFG

Collect all 5 Geography Factbooks!!

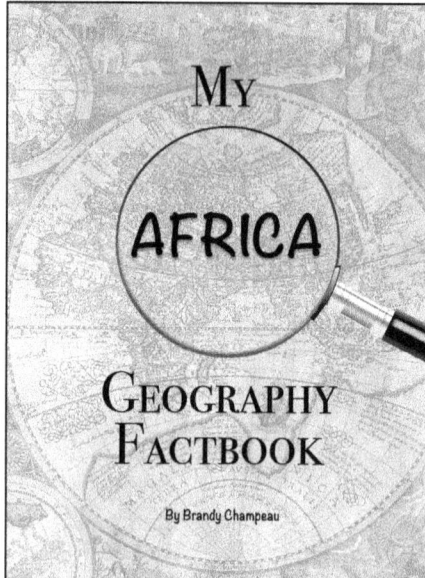

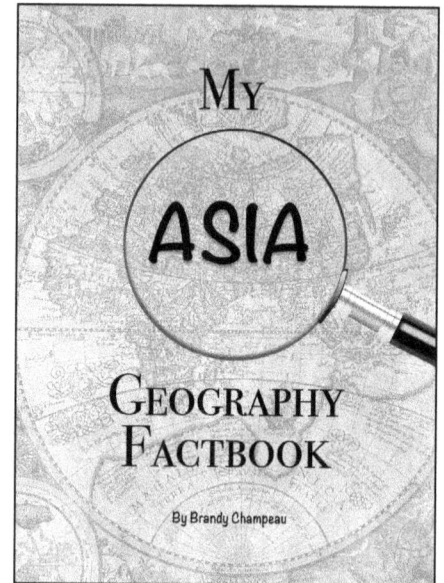

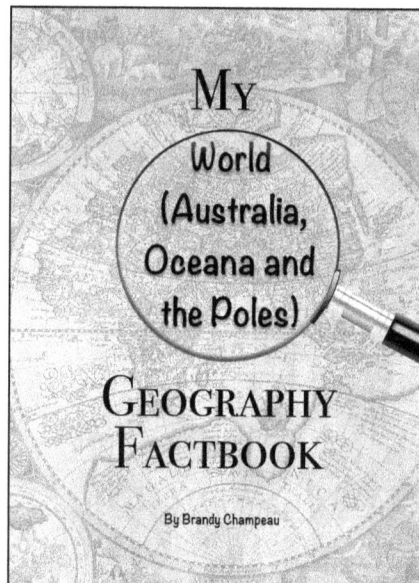

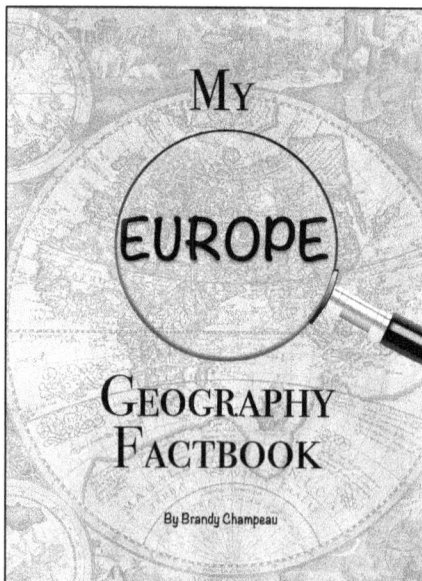

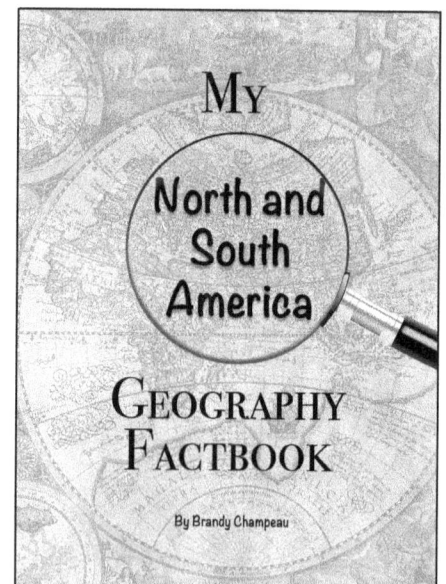

My

AFRICA

GEOGRAPHY
FACTBOOK

By Brandy Champeau

My

ASIA

GEOGRAPHY
FACTBOOK

By Brandy Champeau

My

World
(Australia,
Oceana and
the Poles)

GEOGRAPHY
FACTBOOK

By Brandy Champeau

My

EUROPE

GEOGRAPHY
FACTBOOK

By Brandy Champeau

My

North and
South
America

GEOGRAPHY
FACTBOOK

By Brandy Champeau

Available Now at https://ExploringExpression.com or on
Amazon!!

Introducing Celebrating Today

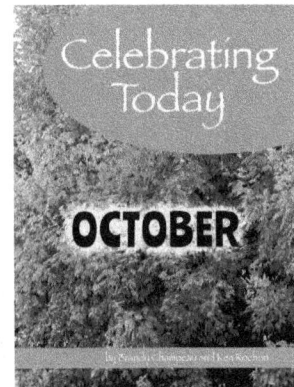

AUGUST

SEPTEMBER

OCTOBER

These books are half journal, half information, and all fun.

Everyday is worth celebrating. It doesn't matter if it is a bad day, a good day or a boring day. It's still worth celebrating simply because you still have today. Every day is a new opportunity for greatness and living your best expression.

So Let's start celebrating - Today!

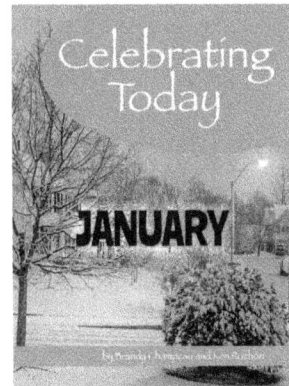

NOVEMBER

DECEMBER

JANUARY

Available Now at https://ExploringExpression.com or on Amazon!!

Also by Brandy Champeau

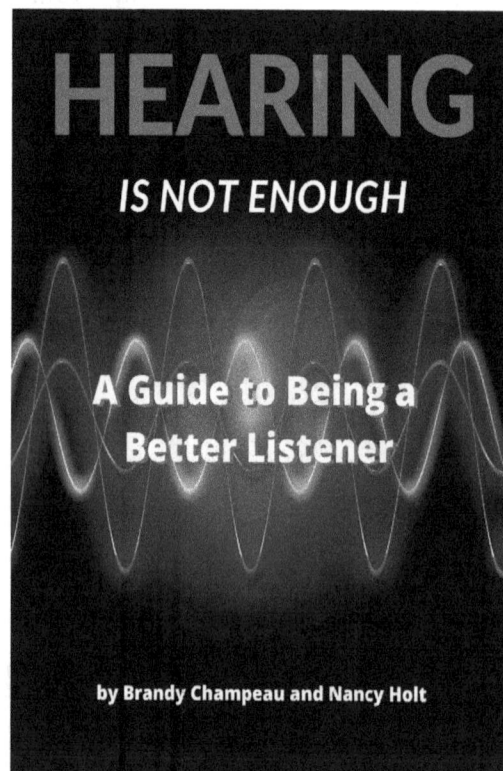

100 THINGS I DIDN'T KNOW BEFORE
MY LEARNING JOURNAL

90 Days To Your Better Expression
A Journal Experience
Brandy Champeau

HEARING
IS NOT ENOUGH

A Guide to Being a Better Listener

by Brandy Champeau and Nancy Holt

Check out these Children's Books and Workbooks by Brandy Champeau.

Available at ExploringExpression.com or on Amazon

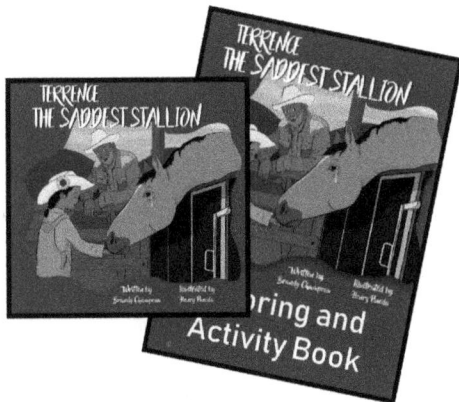